CASUALTIES
OF
CHILDHOOD

A Developmental Perspective
on Sexual Abuse
Using Projective Drawings

Bobbie Kaufman, M.P.S., A.T.R.
& Agnes Wohl, C.S.W., A.C.S.W.

BRUNNER/MAZEL, *Publishers* • NEW YORK

Library of Congress Cataloging-in-Publication Data
Kaufman, Bobbie
    Casualties of childhood : a developmental perspective on sexual
abuse using projective drawings / Bobbie Kaufman and Agnes Wohl.
        p.   cm.
    Includes bibliographical references and index.
    ISBN 0-87630-652-0
    1. Sexually abused children—Mental health.   2. House-Tree-Person
Technique.   3. Kinetic Family Drawing Test.   I. Wohl, Agnes
II. Title.
    [DNLM: 1. Art Therapy.   2. Child Abuse, Sexual—psychology.
3. Child Development Disorders—etiology.   4. Child of Impaired
parents—psychology.   WA 320 K205c]
RJ507.S49K38   1992
618.92′8583—dc20
DNLM/DLC
for Library of Congress   91-40718
                                                                        CIP

Published by
BRUNNER/MAZEL, INC.
19 Union Square West
New York, New York 10003

Manufactured in the United States of America

Designed by Brigid McCarthy

10 9 8 7 6 5 4

CONTENTS

LIST OF DRAWINGS

Please note that all of the drawings presented originally appeared on 8½ × 11 inch sheets of paper. The actual sizes of the drawings have been reduced to accommodate the production requirements of this book; however, the size relationships among the drawings remain consistent. In addition, a number of drawings have been darkened to allow for reproduction.

ACKNOWLEDGMENTS

We are indebted to the children and adults who willingly contributed their drawings for the work of this book. We hope that the pain so explicitly expressed through these drawings will somehow be instrumental in helping to prevent others from enduring the same. Although their names have been changed, their life histories have not.

Special thanks must go to Kate Kane, who has devoted herself to working with sexually abused children and adults and who helped the authors immeasurably by providing invaluable data. Additional words of appreciation go to Kenneth Marion for his assistance in the quantitative analysis of the drawings, and the staff at the Kings Park Psychiatric Center library and Harborfields Public Library for their essential assistance in providing reference materials.

A final expression of gratitude is on a more personal note. Bobbie Kaufman thanks her husband Mal Dankner for his persistent support over the many years of research and writing, despite the sacrifice of countless hours and a sometimes irritable demeanor. She also thanks her children Janice, Michelle, Larry, Allison, and Jay for their continuing support and confidence.

Agnes Wohl is grateful to Howard Kirschen, her husband, for his ongoing encouragement to persevere, his confidence in her abilities, and his critical feedback. Agnes also thanks Gregory, her son, who was born during the writing of this book and who distracted her as little as possible while quietly nursing and playing.

INTRODUCTION

Latency is a difficult time characterized by many demands that are simultaneously placed upon the child. During the normal course of development, youngsters face numerous obstacles. Given healthy constitutions, they are able to cope and incorporate the experiences into their repertoires, utilizing them to enhance their growing abilities to deal with life effectively. Even when confronted with severe problems, a youngster's resilience often shines through. However, when assaulted by trauma, the effects may be profound enough to alter the basic character of the future adult.

Historically, the prevalent belief in society was that youngsters were unaware of and did not have their own reactions to life events. Eth and Pynoos (1985) in their book *Post-Traumatic Stress Disorder in Children* provide a historical perspective on childhood trauma. They identify the early twentieth century as the period when physicians began to recognize that developmental delays were correlated with psychological factors. Up to that time, any harmful effects suffered by the child-victim of trauma were believed to depend, almost exclusively, upon the parental response to the trauma. The 1950s, however, unfolded the recognition of inherent biological differences or the unique strengths and vulnerabilities of each infant. This led to the belief that differing susceptibilities and thresholds for painful occurrences exist within each individual.

DEFINITIONS OF TRAUMA

The *American Heritage Dictionary of the English Language* (1981) defines trauma as "an emotional shock that creates substantial and lasting damage to the psychological development of the individual, generally leading to neurosis" (p. 1366). In the psychiatric literature, trauma has been noted to cause a specific syndrome or grouping of symptoms known as *Post-traumatic Stress Disorder* (PTSD). Van der Kolk (1987) summarized the following key reactions that Kardiner, the first person to describe PTSD, identified as the result of trauma: "1) a persistence of startle response and irritability, 2) proclivity to explosive outbursts of aggression, 3) fixation on the trauma, 4) constriction of the general level of personality functioning, and 5) atypical dream life" (p. 2).

ANALYTIC VIEWS OF TRAUMA

Freud's Definition of Trauma

The analytic community has defined and redefined trauma. Beginning with Freud, this phenomenon was conceived of as an unbearable situation which threatened one's psychic equilibrium. Later, he modified this view believing that unacceptable impulses were aroused by a noxious situation, thereby producing the traumatic effect. Many of Freud's followers believe that it is not the experience itself that has the traumatic effect but rather its revival as a memory after the individual has entered sexual maturity (Furst, 1967). Freud (1926-59), himself, concluded that the most essential predictor about the effect of trauma is the victim's perception of its potential lethality and his or her subjective experience of helplessness—regardless of the objective reality.

Freud also stated that partial traumas cumulatively produce a traumatic effect. "They are part components of a single story of suffering" (Furst, 1967, p. 6). The initial trauma results in a symptom that appears for a short time and is then passed off. Succeeding similar experiences, however, may revive and stabilize the original symptom. Freud believed that although the youngster is not sufficiently developed to be able to understand and incorporate the traumatic event(s), these experiences leave an indelible mark. Even when the partial trauma consists of only one experience, it may trigger an inappropriately strong future response. Whether the trauma consists of one event or many events, the memory of the trauma is repressed but the associated feelings remain conscious, albeit unconnected, to the original event. This state, referred to as isolation of affect and/or dissociation, may result in generalized anxiety. The repressed memories continue to exert their unhealthy influences since there is no opportunity to integrate or work through the emotions that have been aroused.

Anna Freud's Perspective on Trauma

Anna Freud, commenting on trauma in *Psychic Trauma* (Furst, 1967), states that the salient aspects in determining trauma have to do with two factors. The first is concerned with the suddenness of situations for which the individual has no time to prepare psychologically. The second involves a visible result attesting to the disruption of the ego organization. When a person has experienced a trauma, a subsequent alteration of the individual's actions and demeanor are generally discernible. There is a disturbance in the functioning of the ego (i.e., a rigidity of the defenses in terms of their selection and use, and a breakdown in reality testing). The behavioral manifestations of the trauma may be either a virtual catatonic state of being or, conversely, an "emotional storm, accompanied by frenzied, undirected disorganized behavior bordering on panic" (Furst, 1967, p. 40). This state of dysfunction may last from moments to months; recovery may be immediate, may take place over a period of time, or may never occur.

Shengold's View on Trauma

A major consequence of the breakdown of ego functions resulting from trauma is a state in which the child dissociates from the traumatizing event and loses contact with her or himself in the process. In a sense, the child's soul is destroyed. To so "deform a soul takes chronic and repeated abuse" (Shengold, 1979, p. 551). Children, who are more fragile than adults, are especially vulnerable to "soul murder," which Shengold defines as situations in which a child is repeatedly and intentionally presented with toxic events that alternate with emotional neglect. These circumstances organize the defenses, the id, ego, and superego structures, the developmental process, and the personality. When one person uses his or her position to dominate another in order to squelch the other's uniqueness, integrity, and feelings, the result is an interference in the victim's ability to use logical thought and remain reality based. The victim's sense of identity is thereby profoundly altered.

Often trauma involves so potent an inundation of toxins that the psyche is unable to cope. This triggers a barrage of emotions which strike terror and result in a mutation of the youngster's previous defensive structure, range of affective responses, and cognitive processes. Moreover, the repetitive, amnesia-like states the child unconsciously invokes for psychological survival causes estrangement from his or her sense of self and also increases the potential for robotlike and overly compliant behavior.

SELF PSYCHOLOGY VIEWS ON TRAUMA

What Is Trauma?

The school of self psychology evolved its own theories on trauma. Ulman and Brothers (1988) believe that a trauma is based on an actual event whose subjective meaning disorganizes the fantasies of the self and changes the view of the self in an untenable manner. Krystal (1988), focusing his attention on the internal experience of the trauma and its concomitant affects, concludes that trauma produces an insufferable affective state which potentially threatens to disrupt and even decimate ego functions.

The classical analytic position on trauma as espoused by the Freuds and others maintains that the experience of trauma is not the actual occurrence but rather the internal experience of the event. However, contemporary analysts such as Ulman and Brothers (1988) believe that trauma is based "on real occurrences that have, as their unconscious meaning, the shattering of central organizing fantasies of self in relation to self object" (front jacket). It is their contention that the meaning of an event changes an individual's experience of himself in ways that are unbearable.

Shattering of the Self

Trauma has the capacity to induce a shattering of the child's fantasies of self and of the child's sense of omnipotence and invulnerability. Moreover, when a youngster is subjected to a single traumatic event or series of such occurrences, he or she tries to make sense of the situation. To do so the child creates fantasy explanations and activates any or all available defense maneuvers. Ulman and Brothers (1988) believe that a person develops "meaning structures" — ways by which the person experiences him or herself in relation to others. Fantasies are developed in relation to these structures and serve an organizing function for the individual. When a noxious event, such as sexual abuse, occurs, a variety of adaptive mechanisms are disrupted. The trauma "shatters the self (which is) a multidimensional psychological construct reflecting the subject's experience of mental being and physical existence" (p. 5). Traumatic symptoms such as those identified in the DSM-III-R (1987) under Post-traumatic Stress Disorder (i.e., flashbacks, nightmares) are manifested and signal the "shattering and faulty restitution of the meaning structures" (Ulman & Brothers, 1988, p. 3).

Once the self is shattered, there is a frantic attempt at reconstitution for the trauma has challenged "the self as a center for organizing activities" (Ulman & Brothers, 1988, p. 7). As a consequence of the youngster's inability to gain mastery over the noxious occurrence and the subsequent disillusionment of his or her omnipotence, the youngster feels like a failure. In addition, one of the consequences of a traumatic event is that the child's early and essential fantasies, which are normatively of a grandiose and potent self, are disrupted. These illusions of self power are pivotal antecedents to the development of a healthy personality organization. However, in instances of trauma, as opposed to normality, they are not gradually transformed into an authentic feeling of a sense of strength within the environment. The traumatic state interferes with this transformation. The effect of trauma is such that youngsters will experience themselves as impotent and unrelated to their actions.

The Shattering of Assumptions

Janoff-Bulman (1985 cited in Ulman & Brothers, 1988) believes that trauma is made up of "the shattering of any one of three basic assumptions about self and the world ... (1) the belief in personal invulnerability; (2) the perception of the world as meaningful and comprehensible; and (3) the view of oneself in a positive light" (p. 21). When a harmful, nonsensical event happens in a child's life and the youngster tries to understand it as "meaningful and comprehensible," there is an off-centering of reality and an induced state of cognitive dissonance. In order to rectify this, the child's view of him or herself must be sacrificed at the cost of self-esteem or the child must relinquish his or her view of the world as a place he or she can understand.

Alterations of Affects

From Krystal's (1988) vantage point, trauma causes children to undergo a permanent change in their affective lives. The emotions evoked during a trauma are overwhelming to children. In an attempt to cope, they become numb to their own feelings. As a result, their affects are converted into psychosomatic symptoms and other problems. Additionally, a state of helplessness is aroused in which youngsters give up, yielding to the danger. They no longer feel anxious because emotions are blocked. In a sense, the child has murdered an integral part of the self and a state of passivity ensues. This passivity, however, is not without consequences. When children experience themselves as totally helpless, it changes their self-perception and their perceptions of the world permanently. This leads to feelings of shame and a lifestyle of despair.

There is an interesting juxtaposition here. For while the child has been initially able to achieve a feeling of relief from the trauma by cutting off his or her emotions, this state "is also the first part of dying" (Krystal, 1988, p. 102). Krystal explains this comment by stating that children's capacity to initiate activities and use their minds for survival are also sacrificed. Paradoxically, this state is called upon to help self-preservation, both physically and psychologically. Once a child has been sexually misused, particularly by a trusted caretaker, development will be drastically transformed. The child's sense of self, affects, experience of the world, and innocence are lost—never to be retrieved in quite the same manner.

THE TRAUMA OF SEXUAL ABUSE

Child sexual abuse is a multifaceted issue on the intrapsychic, familial, and societal level. It is only recently that our society has acknowledged the scope of this problem and has tried to understand the causes and effects it has on the victim and on society as a whole. It is an issue that stirs our most primitive instincts and evokes feelings of helplessness, rage, and repulsion. Reflecting one of the darkest sides of childhood experiences, the effects of this trauma reverberate throughout the life cycle of the individual and play out in the dynamics of the family for generations.

Much research has been devoted to the topics of childhood development and the sexual abuse of youngsters. Significantly less attention has been given to the specific developmental effects of this abuse. Finkelhor (1986) concludes that latency (ages 5 to 10 or 11) appears to be the most common time for the onset of sexual abuse. Paradoxically, this is also the time the child is expected to develop inner controls over instincts and to divert energies to incorporate the mores, values, and ethos of society.

Casualties of Childhood examines sexual abuse from a developmental perspective. Normative latency goals, tasks, and expectations are explored with an eye towards understanding the consequences of this desecration upon the child. It is clear that the experience of sexual abuse and the resulting psychic trauma cause the derailment of normal latency development in most youngsters.

The victim of childhood sexual abuse frequently has difficulty revealing the mishandling. Despite this, and paradoxically because of it, a constellation of symptoms suggesting sexual abuse often goes unexplained. In other situations, symptoms suggestive of sexual exploitation may be recognized but remain unconfirmed because no validation methodology exists. As such, alternate modes of assessment have been sought by the professional community. One of these has been the utilization of drawings as an efficacious diagnostic tool to communicate the unspoken (Hammer, 1980).

This book will examine the effects of sexual abuse of latency-age children as reflected in the drawings of both abused children and adult survivors. Specifically, the House, Tree, Person, and Kinetic Family Drawings will be studied from the perspective of consequences on the development of youngsters' ego, superego, and object relations. We will also present the long-term effects of sexual molestation as projected in the drawings of adults who were sexually victimized as latency children.

A CRY FROM THE ABUSED

Sexual abuse is the ultimate form of being used
It is a denial of self with all rights refused
It means that when they are through
I can't even trust myself, the abuser or you
It means giving up a part
Of me—a part of my heart
It takes away from my will to survive
From my innermost purpose of being alive
It makes me doubt why you even care
In fact, it makes me question everything—everywhere
I feel like giving up the last thing I have
The hope instilled by God above
The unconditional love,
Life's philosophy seems like it's been taken from me
I often wish restitution
Or anything that might be a resolution
I need an answer, whole or in part,
To stop the aching in my heart
I want once more to forgive
And to pass from this stage and live
To be free from the weights
And the semicomatose states
To be loosed from the guilt and reason
And to know the abuse only lasted for a season

—*Anonymous Sexual Abuse Survivor*

CASUALTIES

OF

CHILDHOOD

A Developmental Perspective
on Sexual Abuse
Using Projective Drawings

CHAPTER 1

PARADIGMS OF TRAUMA
AND SEXUAL ABUSE

Neither child sexual abuse nor the specific category of incest are diagnostic categories. They are not included in the DSM-III-R although some have argued that just as Post-traumatic Stress Disorder has its own particular criteria and diagnostic code, so should child sexual abuse. A number of professionals, in fact, have identified a designated set of behavioral indicators and symptoms, labeling them *Child Sexual Abuse Syndrome*. Within this construct, sexual abuse is viewed as an external event that triggers an internal process with a range of symptoms and characteristics, which are predictable regardless of other influencing factors.

We subscribe to the perspective that incest is an external event which is incorporated within the context of the child's premorbid personality, stage of development, physical and psychological constitution, experience of previous traumas, and familial environment. The identification of the perpetrator and the family's and society's response (i.e., courts, police) to the abuse are also significant factors. It is the interweaving of these components that determines the symptom picture and future direction of the youngster's developing personality.

IS SEXUAL ABUSE HARMFUL?

Yates (1982) reviewed literature written in the 1960s and 1970s concerned with the question of whether or not the incestuous relationship is deleterious for the child. Stating that it may be erroneous to assume that the child has been negatively effected, Yates concludes that the abuse may provide a source of nurturance not otherwise available to the child. She maintains that the child may miss opportunities to disclose the abuse partly because of a reluctance to give up the gratification received from the special nature of the connection.

Others (Butler, 1978; Forward & Buck, 1978) believe that neglected youngsters may derive positive benefits from the incestuous relationship without which an environment of desolation would continue. They espouse that the incestuous contact, which may be the only nurturance, affection, or attention the victim has ever known, can function to help the child feel loved. Shengold (1980), however, wonders whether such a connection, which leads to the future sexualization of relationships, is better or worse than the developmental arrests created by deprivation. He maintains it may appear that the child is seeking the sexual relationship, when it is the longing for closeness that he craves. The emotional cost to the youngster is severe impairment that outweighs any benefits. As stated by Ferenczi (1949), "when love of a different kind from that which they need is forced upon children in the stage of tenderness, it may lead to pathological consequences" (p. 228).

Summit (1983) concurs and views incest as having severe repercussions in youngsters' development. Based on his clinical experience, he postulates that children forfeit themselves by participating in a sexually abusive relationship through a process he defines as the "Child Sexual Abuse Accommodation Syndrome." Children also may not make attempts to end the abuse because they are cognizant and fearful of the consequences of disclosure. An alternate explanation for "keeping the secret" is that youngsters often form an identification with their abusers. Any exploration or revival of the memories of the event inevitably point to the perpetrator's badness. This, in turn, generates concomitant feelings of badness in the victim.

Finkelhor and Browne (1985) developed a model about the impact of sexual abuse, fully asserting that it is not only harmful but devastating. They identify four areas affected by this violation, namely, traumatic sexualization, betrayal, powerlessness, and stigmatization. These categories point to resultant difficulties within the child and the child's view of others.

Another major contributor to child sexual abuse (CSA) research is Suzanne Sgroi (1982, 1988), whose extensive work with sexually abused victims has repeatedly emphasized the problems manifested by these children resulting from the sexual encounters. She has been preeminent in identifying the behavioral indicators of sexual abuse and the sequential patterns within which this abuse takes place. The question of damage is virtually a moot point for her. Her direct experience in interviewing thousands of youngsters has proven time and again the preponderance of deleterious effects.

Clearly, and as this volume will demonstrate, the effect of sexual abuse is profound; it produces a major alteration to the self. Evidence of this is seen in the ego's damaged capacity to modulate impulses, utilize defenses, test reality, and moderate superego and id demands. Relationships are often tainted with the ghosts of the event. Consequently, innocent acts of others may be interpreted as attacks on the self. Others become viewed in a distorted manner. All hope of satisfying relationships may be lost. Unquestionably, the power this trauma exerts on the developing personality and character of the child is penetrating.

SYMPTOM FORMATION

Sexual abuse is an act that breaks through the stimulus barrier of the ego, floods the youngster with anxiety, and renders him or her unable to cope.

Often the victim is seen diagnostically with symptoms that are characteristic of Post-traumatic Stress Disorder. More alarmingly, victims often exhibit traits of character pathology such as narcissism, paranoia, dysthymia, and borderline, or even psychosis.

Symptoms manifested by these individuals have been widely discussed in professional articles and books. Most writers agree that there are both immediate and chronic symptoms for the majority of sexual abuse victims with general data supporting the hypothesis that emotional disturbances appear to be most severe when the abuse commences at an early age and continues through later stages (Brooks, 1985).

Browne and Finklehor (1986) summarize the immediate aftermath (within two years) as including eating and sleeping disturbances, fears and phobias, depression, guilt, shame, anger, and school problems. They highlight that short-term deleterious effects are mainly of the internal nature such as those reflected in depression rather than in aggression. Peters (1978) notes that there are significant changes in sleeping patterns with a considerable number of nightmares reported. Victims also acknowledge fears of being abandoned and experiencing disturbed eating patterns.

Psychosomatic symptoms also appear to be prevalent among sexually abused victims (Forward & Buck, 1978; Kaufman, Peck, & Tagiuri, 1954). These may include migraines, gastrointestinal disturbances, dizziness, skin disorders, and other debilitating aches and pains. Everstine and Everstine (1989) concur with these conclusions and add alterations in toileting patterns such as enuresis to the list of symptoms. It is as if these victims are more psychologically prepared to deal with the physical pain and discomfort than to face the emotional tensions, anxiety, and conflicts associated with the abuse. They express their distress through their bodies.

Of serious concern is the emergence of a number of psychoticlike symptoms which may appear in various combinations in different children. Among these are hallucinations, delusions, and recurrent and obsessional thoughts, some of which may reach psychotic proportions. Additionally, a breakdown of reality testing and logical thinking ensues (Gelinas, 1983). A state of dissociation, in which the victim consciously induces some type of self-hypnotic anesthesia to avoid the stimuli of the trauma, is also common (Gelinas, 1983).

Cognition is another area impacted upon by the sexual exploitation. One way this type of dysfunction becomes apparent is through school performance. While some sexually abused children seem to excel in this area (Sgroi, 1982) as it is their only haven, others show serious learning problems which may take the form of concentration and attention difficulties (Butler, 1978). It may be that there are intrusive thoughts or overwhelming feelings of anxiety that interfere with the child's ability to attend to the classwork.

Relational disturbances are frequently noted, particularly in incest victims. Peer interactions are thwarted partly because the preoccupation with sexual impulses has the propensity to isolate the youngster. This preoccupation may result from the physical pleasure invoked by the sexual activity between the adult and child since it often becomes intrinsically reinforcing (Yates, 1982). Ongoing sexual behavior may be the youngster's way of reenacting some aspect of the trauma to gain control over the associated anxiety. As such, it is difficult to redirect the child away from the sexual activity to more age-appropriate satisfactions. Yates writes that these youngsters are unable to distinguish between sexual and nonsexual relationships. As a result, the role of sexuality in intimate relationships becomes a blurry issue for the sexually abused child.

Finkelhor and Browne (1985), as noted earlier, identify "traumatic sexualization" as one of the four traumagenic reactions to CSA. They describe a child's sexuality as being developmentally derailed as a result of sexual assault. The youngster gains love and rewards for his or her sexual activity; the child's sexual organs are given enormous significance and the child, in turn, comes to value them inappropriately. The offender's communications about sexual mores exacerbate the value of the sexual organs and create a sense of bewilderment in the child about sexual norms. Out of confusion, the youngster may subsequently attempt to engage peers in similar sexual behavior (a form of repetition compulsion), frightening them and causing the others to avoid him or her.

Many authors (Brooks, 1985; Everstine & Everstine, 1989; Katan, 1973; Kaufman, Peck, & Tagiuri, 1954) note that victims of sexual abuse also have a disturbance in the area of sexual identity formation. The victimization skews their sense of sexuality. Their understanding of sexual roles becomes distorted. Some female children tend to identify with the abuser and focus on the acquisition of the penis. The absence of this organ creates a feeling of being damaged. The victim comes to prefer a male identity which is seen as undamaged and powerful. In instances when the attacker of a male is also a male, the victim's sense of manhood may well be threatened. Experiencing himself as powerless and weak, as well as the recipient of the penis, he may begin to identify with a female role. He may believe that through his passivity he will please the perpetrator and thereby ward off further aggression. Whether the victim and the offender are the same or opposite sex may also effect the victim's sexual identity. Some studies have linked homosexuality and prostitution to a history of sexual abuse (Ochberg, 1988). This whole area is worthy of more in-depth study.

Self-destructive behavior as a by-product of CSA is noted throughout the literature (Brothers, 1982; Finkelhor & Browne, 1986; Sgroi, 1982; Shapiro, 1987). Often the victim's need for self-punishment, as a response to feeling guilty and bad, leads to such behaviors. At other times, pain is self-induced to counter the feelings of numbness and deadness. Some victims masturbate compulsively and excessively, often to the point of self-injury. Incest victims are frequently filled with suicidal ideation and may attempt suicide. Delinquent behaviors, and those carried to a more extreme level, as identified in the DSM-III-R under Conduct Disorders, have also been identified as part of the consequences of the abuse.

Development of a Borderline Core

Children who have been sexually abused by trusted caretakers, upon whom they are dependent, find their basic concept of self and the world severely shaken. The youngster's character structure, self-image, self-esteem, and trust in self and others take on new and different forms. In a sense, the child who existed prior to the trauma has been murdered; a new child emerges who may be jaded and damaged. Shapiro (1987) suggests a relationship between incest and the borderline personality organization. The Everstines (1989) also point out that childhood sexual trauma can be linked to Borderline Personality Disorder. The rudiments of the main characteristics of the Borderline Personality Disorder, namely, poor impulse control, high anxiety, acting-out behaviors, splitting, intensification of aggression, and sublimation difficulties, are often manifested in the symptom picture of the sexually abused child. Impulse control problems are frequently introjected from parental perpetrators who, by the very act of sexual exploitation, model acting out. In addition, the aggressive and libidinal drives to which the perpetrator yields are also stimulated in the child, negating the possibility that the youngster can sublimate them.

As a result of sexual victimization, particularly molestation that is ongoing, the youngster's ego becomes flooded with anxiety and his or her impulse control becomes increasingly tenuous. Generally, part of the function of an introject is to support such controls and to provide self-soothing functions. In order to maintain a positive internalized image of the exploiter and/or the nonoffending parent, the child begins to separate or split apart positive and negative attributes. This functions to ward off more widespread anxiety and to preserve the integrity of the ego, upon whose foundation are built positive introjects and internalizations. The splitting safeguards the youngster's ego by separating out the parts of the introjected parent that represent the conflict created by the sexual abuse.

Mood Disturbances

An important, if not essential, area of human experience acutely affected by sexual abuse is the arena of emotions. This is where we experience the fullness and breadth of our humanness. For the sexually abused child, the world of feelings often becomes constricted and diminished. Although clinicians have historically felt that childhood depression is a rare situation, within the last 25 years it has been acknowledged.

Symonds (1966) believes that depressive states in children are expressed through their behavior. Sad youngsters do not act sad; they act bad. Psonanski and Srull (1970, cited in Chess & Hassibi, 1981) identify the following criteria for childhood depression: feeling sad and unhappy with episodic crying; apathy; withdrawal; disturbed sleep; feeling rejected and unloved; low self-esteem; negative self-image; and self-destructive ideation.

Depression, frequently chronic, is the single most common response to childhood incest (Browne & Finkelhor, 1986). Sexually misused children exhibit a typical depressive symptom picture. They are filled with somatic concerns including hypochondria, headaches, and stomachaches. Helplessness is also a very immediate experience for them. The abused child becomes overpowered by the adult and is left feeling fearful and anxious. Due to the youngster's inability to stop the molestation, an impaired sense of efficacy develops, which is often "associated with . . . despair, depression, and even suicidal behavior" (Finkelhor & Brown, 1985, p. 536). Guilt is a common reaction to the abuse, feeding back into feelings of depression and loathsomeness.

Another major consequence of the sexual exploitation is the child's limited ability to experience a full range of emotions. In attempting to close the door on the intolerable feelings elicited from the abuse, the child inadvertently blocks an avenue that allows entry of positive feelings. More alarmingly, the youngster experiences a deadness, a total emotional void. Krystal (1988) writes about "alexithymia," an inability to differentiate affects, psychological numbness, or general affective disturbance. He states that trauma causes a regression in the ability to express emotions.

Freud (1926/1953) remarks that the actual danger in a situation is unimportant in relation to this syndrome, for it is the victim's subjective evaluation of the peril that determines the psychological sequelae. Sexually abused youngsters often fear for their lives despite the presence or absence of actual threats. When youngsters feel helpless, they give up. Their emotions, which at that point, are too painful and overwhelming, propel them to repress their feelings and thereby relinquish part of their selves. Their anxiety and excitation change to surrender and passivity; they experience either no feelings or, at the most, vague, diffuse, and undefined emotional sensations.

The consequences of this go beyond the obvious. We use our emotions to help monitor or evaluate ourselves, to provide signals to generate specific behaviors and to set a path of direction for actions. Alexithymics are unable to differentiate between such emotions as happiness, sadness, hunger, or exhaustion and, instead, have a general sense of discomfort which they are unable to specify. Their affects are often expressed somatically and are manifested through an array of physical problems.

RUPTURED TRUST

As mentioned previously, one of the most profound and universal impacts of sexual abuse is the disintegration of the children's sense of trust in themselves and in the adults upon whom they depend. *The American Heritage Dictionary of the English Language* (1981) defines trust as "firm reliance on the integrity, ability or character of a person or thing; confident belief; faith" (p. 1378). Erikson (1963) believes that a state of trust implies "that one has learned to rely on the sameness and continuity of the outer providers . . . [and] also that one may trust oneself and the capacity of one's own organs to cope with urges" (p. 248). Trust both in the environment and in oneself develop simultaneously throughout the life cycle, changing and modifying as a result of one's experiences. Brothers (1982) delineates the aspects of each of these areas. The development of the ability to trust others includes experiencing others as decent, helpful, unselfish, compassionate, shielding, dependable, and responsible and nonabusive of another's deficits. Varying levels of trust develop in children based on their individual experiences. A sense of trust is an evolving process influenced by life events (Erikson, 1963).

Trust in Others

Brothers (1982) has found that while the effect on the child's trust of others may be either heightened or diminished as a result of sexual exploitation, very frequently there is inflated trust in others. She explains that this paradoxical reaction may represent the victim's attempt to protect the trusted perpetrator in order to maintain his or her own ability to trust the outside world upon which the victim is vitally dependent. Acknowledging the malevolence of the perpetrator would otherwise cause the child to withdraw from others at a time when they are most needed. The need to hold others in high regard and also continue intimate relationships is so strong that the victim will often sacrifice his or her own integrity to do so.

Incest, in particular, occurs within a relationship that is supposed to be based on care, protection, and nurturance for the youngster. It is a place where the child should be able to receive an understanding of reality and relationships. In fact, "incest is a profound abandonment and betrayal, a travesty of the parental love and care that is a young child's inherent right" (Gelinas, 1983, p. 319).

Trust exists along a continuum within which a paranoid disorder can be seen as representing the most extreme rupture. Its hallmarks are extreme suspicion, feelings of persecution, secrecy, grandiosity, hypersensitivity, and the overuse of the defenses of externalization and projection. As such, it is understandable that a sexually abused child would begin to develop paranoid traits or styles of relating. The world has been experienced as unsafe, malevolent, and uncontrollable. The child may have also apprehended the abuse as retribution for being "bad" in some shape or form. The youngster's identity becomes that of a victim who has little control over his or her life. Therefore, while the suspiciousness the child initially develops in reaction to the abuse is warranted, if it becomes overly generalized, it can lead to paranoia.

Self-trust

Self-trust is composed of the ability to modulate one's affects, use good judgment, set realistic goals, manage anxiety, experience the self as lovable, have the ability to comfort and empathize with one's self, and, last, work towards self-realization (Brothers, 1982). When children are victims to sexual assault they feel physically and morally helpless because their personalities are not sufficiently developed to resist or trust their own perceptions in relation to the abuse (Ferenczi, 1949). As such, the path towards self-realization becomes encumbered; their sense of self-trust becomes mutilated.

Brothers (1982) found evidence to substantiate that a problem in trust "is a key element in the aftermath of . . . incest" (p. 144). We note that this supports Ferenczi's (1949) comments that a child who has been sexually abused no longer "trusts his own senses." After the exploitation has occurred, the abuser often acts as if nothing has happened. The child becomes psychologically and sometimes physically injured. Yet, since there is no external validation of the internal experience, the child begins to doubt his or her own judgments. In addition, the perpetrator squashes the child's sense of self and self-trust (Shengold, 1979). With time, the perpetrator's distorted perceptions become those of the child.

The inability to trust oneself and others as a consequence of sexual abuse has profound implications which reflect the youngster's shattered construct regarding the world and his or her self. Future relationships are colored and marred by the trauma. The child who is unable to trust is also more likely to be unhappy, conflicted, and unpopular with his peers and generally maladjusted (Rotter [1980] cited in Brothers, 1982). The implications of being sexually assaulted resonate throughout the child's very being.

MUTILATION OF SELF-ESTEEM

A complaint that is virtually universal in sexual abuse victims is the intense feeling of being abnormal and damaged. Yet, as Reich (1979) states, "a positive evaluation of the self ... is a pre-condition for one's well-being" (p. 215). Feelings of self-respect inherent in self-esteem are absent in the findings of Lusk and Waterman (cited in MacFarlane, Waterman, & Conerly et al., 1986), who identify low self-esteem as one of the most frequent sequelae of CSA. Citing numerous authors they support that poor self-esteem, an injured and inadequate sense of self, negative self-image, and poor self-identity result from sexual abuse. Katan (1973) found that a common denominator among her incested patients was "unbelievably low self-esteem" (p. 220). Brothers (1982), using objective measurements, compared incest victims with others in a control group. She found that the sexually abused group scored statistically significantly lower on ratings of self-esteem.

Sgroi (1982) attributes low self-esteem to the fear of being physically damaged or "spoiled." Feelings of guilt and blame for being involved in the sexual relationship as well as guilt over the consequences following disclosure all contribute to the child's poor self-image. Finkelhor and Browne (1985) conclude that low self-esteem derives from the attitudes of others which victims internalize over time. A message is communicated to them, either directly or subvertly, that they are damaged goods.

Jacobson (1954) believes that self-esteem is dependent upon the positive comparison between one's vision of oneself and one's ego ideal. The capacity to adequately live up to the expectations of one's superego is a mature method of regulating self-esteem (Reich, 1973). Yet "guilt, shame, a negative self-image ... are part of the inheritance of the sexually abused child" (Shapiro, 1987, p. 47). Various theoreticians postulate that a youngster tries to avoid disappointment and the resulting frustration by living up to the ideal self and experiences shame when he is unable to do so (Kohut, 1966). Since sexually abused child-victims are generally unable to ward off the attacks, despite what they may believe are omens or warnings, they generally feel like they failed themselves. Moreover, they perceive themselves as defective. This culminates in intense feelings of shame and marred self-esteem.

CONCLUSION

There appears to be little doubt that sexual abuse is a trauma that leaves some mark on all youngsters upon whom it is foisted. Each child, depending on a wide range of factors, endeavors to cope with the sexual interactions through whatever means available, struggling to make it fit into a construct that makes sense and allows him or her to continue being. Despite these attempts, and also because of them, the exploitation dramatically alters the person who was there before.

The effect of trauma, and specifically the trauma of sexual molestation, leads to the creation of a dissociative state, which involves depersonalized feelings, psychological numbing, and other mechanisms developed by children to distance themselves from the intolerable state of being. They become detached from their own affects and experience a psychological death or "soul murder." They no longer know what they feel, think, or who their sense of self is. The self, according to Pine (1982), is "the experience of a sense of ownership . . . the source of an urge, an effector or action, or a center of experience" (p. 143-144). This is in contrast to the "it," which is experienced as acting on the "I" or self and is disowned. The self is the integration of the "I" and the "we" (Strechler cited in Tolpin, 1971). Essential to this concept is the continuity of experience in one's life, present and future expectations.

Experiences that are familiar become "mine" and are seen as part of "me." Initially, sexual abuse is felt to be coming from an outside source, or from the "it." The abuse impinges on the self, creating conflict and dissonance. As this occurrence happens again and again, which is the predominant scenario in abuse (Sgroi, 1982; Summit, 1983), it takes on a familiar tone. Over time, this familiarity tends to reduce the level of dissonance and enables the experience to become integrated into the self. The abuse is no longer felt as belonging to "it," but rather the abuse has become part of the "me." As such, when youngsters are assaulted, they become prone to seeing themselves as victims and expect to be put in this position continually, consciously foregoing any sense of power or control. The abuse thus becomes incorporated into the basic aspects of the self; youngsters' identity and experience of themselves become linked to the sexual acts foisted upon them.

The cost of the ego maneuvers sexually assaulted youngsters deploy for their survival is that of relinquishing their sense of self as good, worthy, and powerful people. There are times when children will present themselves as symptom-free. However, just as there may be a delayed onset of overt signs in Post-traumatic Stress Disorder, this is also true for child-victims of sexual assault. Psychiatric disturbances may not immediately emerge but may manifest at a later date (Albright & Reice, 1986). Molested children may appear as though they are coping well but this may, in fact, mask isolation of affect (Meiselman, 1978). The Everstines (1989) found that children who are seemingly unaffected by the abuse are at greater risk for developing more severe pathology as adults than youngsters who display initial problems.

The bottomline is that sexual abuse cannot be ignored away, no matter how hard the child tries. The marks of abuse are etched into the child's basic character. These scars will be seen in the child's developing ego and superego, as well as in his or her ability to relate to others. The remainder of this book will attempt to provide readers with a guide as to how these scars surface in projective drawings of sexually violated children, and in adult survivors of latency-age sexual abuse.

CHAPTER 2

GENERAL PRINCIPLES IN THE ANALYSIS OF PROJECTIVE DRAWINGS

Since earliest times, drawings have been used as a tool to express how the world is experienced. Prehistoric man drew pictures of animals on cave walls to depict and reflect his environment. The American Indians carved images into mountain walls to portray their fear and wonder of the world. The ancient Egyptians created elaborate murals detailing life as they lived and understood it. Thousands of years later, contemporary man looks at these varied and wonderful drawings and comprehends the world of ancient man through his art. But when we look at the vibrant colors and carefully angled lines, we don't simply see a picture, we feel what these men and women felt about their lives millenniums ago. We know it in an intuitive, affective way. We feel the order and the careful rhythms.

Moreover, although these creations reflect the greater cultural values and standards of these periods, they also communicate each artist's experience of society. Individual differences are revealed through the drawings and tell us about the creator's inner world. The choice of subject, the colors, line quality, and the proportion of various objects and people are all symbolic messages from the artist. These metaphoric communications are less subject to censorship than words. Much like dreams they emanate from within and, as such, the symbols selected and the manner of presentation alert the viewer to personally powerful themes and issues.

In the late 1800s, as the field of psychology was evolving, drawings began to be of interest in understanding the mind. An article appeared in Europe correlating children's artwork to their developmental stages (Koppitz, 1968). Eventually, articles and research emerged in the fields of psychiatry and psychology identifying the standardized use of various drawings for intelligence and personality assessment. This began with Goodenough, in the 1920s, who developed an intelligence test based solely on the scoring of drawings. The scoring included such factors as the presence or absence of two-dimensional

13

features, as well as the inclusion and omission of details. Goodenough also pointed the way to future research on children's drawings by calling attention to the possibility that youngsters' personalities, emotions, and conflicts might be revealed through these renderings (Harris, 1963). Focus on the use of drawings as "projective" instruments to understand the individual's underlying dynamics began in earnest in the 1940s by Machover (1949), followed by Levy (1950), Jolles (1952), Hammer (1953), and Buck (1981).

THE RELIABILITY AND VALIDITY OF DRAWINGS AS A PROJECTIVE TOOL

Research on Human Figure Drawings (HFD)

Clinicians have long recognized the significance of symbolic messages in drawings and have sought to confirm clinical observations with hard research. Machover (1949), interested in the contribution that the HFD could offer as a tool for personality assessment, developed indices to measure emotional functioning. In 1968, Koppitz completed a major study to standardize both emotional and developmental indices in the HFD. She created one scoring system which flagged potential emotional difficulties and another which identified normative developmental items for children between the ages of 5 to 12. Hammer (1968) identified a number of researchers who had explored the relationship between specific individual abnormalities and drawings. Kotkov and Goodman (1953), who analyzed the body image of obese woman as mirrored in their drawings, discovered that their renderings were larger and wider compared to a control group of average weight women. In a second example, Machover (1949) noticed that the drawings of hearing impaired individuals emphasized ears. Bender (1952) found that physically impaired children graphically depicted their liabilities.

Additional Individual Drawings Used as Projective Tools

Along with the focus on the HFD/DAP emerged an interest in other subject matter including houses, trees, and families. Markham (1954) investigated items identified in House Drawings created by children and identified a number of normative elements in these drawings. She also suggested that this test might be useful in discriminating between gross intellectual differences. Kellogg (1970) more recently studied thousands of children's House Drawings, looking at developmental aspects. She concluded that there are typical progressive styles in the drawings of all children, despite cultural diversities.

Should Projective Drawings Be Used?

An important aspect to weigh in considering the viability of drawings as projective assessments is the prominent role that visual imagery plays in our internal organization. Arieti (1976) states that "images . . . constitute the foundation of inner reality . . ." (p. 45). The creation of an image is the way an individual tries to replicate the outer objects of his or her experiences. Visual images represent an accumulation of previous perceptions; they are inner portrayals and constructs built on the fragments of memories. Importantly, although images are related to actual external experience, they are not exact replicas. Rather, they are colored by the needs, wishes, and longings of the image producer. As such, a method that can concretize the world of one's images concomitantly offers an avenue into one's internal life. Drawings are a natural outgrowth towards this end.

Harris (1963), who researched the role of drawings in understanding internal processes, believes the formation of concepts and the organization of perception are clearly represented in graphics. Hammer (1980), expanding upon the application of drawings, stresses their essential role within the battery of projective tests. Most psychologists use projective drawings as part of their standard series of tests. Additionally, the information yielded is utilized by art therapists and other psychotherapists as an integral way to cull a comprehensive picture of the patient. Projective drawings, when used in a systematic way, provide invaluable and fruitful material. They are a road into the unconscious; they are metaphors graphically imaging defenses, drives, fears, wishes, motivations, personality styles, strengths and fragilities.

DEVELOPMENTAL ASPECTS OF DRAWING SKILLS

Historical Perspective

As with any other skill or capacity, the ability to draw follows a specific epigenetic developmental sequence. As noted earlier in this chapter, the study of drawings originated in Europe in the late 1800s with an interest in how maturational stages might be reflected in the artwork. Over time, this interest became more sophisticated in its breadth. Rouma (1913), working in France, was the first to establish a progressive sequence to drawing. He delineated a "preliminary stage" which involved the child (1) learning to manipulate an instrument; (2) endowing a rendering with meaning; (3) planning what to draw; and (4) perceiving a likeness between the creation and an actual item.

The Scribble

The scribble is the child's first rendering. It is a non-goal-directed marking utilized primarily for motor expression. Kellogg (1970), an art educator, studied thousands of scribbles created by children ages 2 to 5. She identified 20 "basic scribbles"—unplanned drawing gestures, created both with and without the benefit of eye control, which are common to children the world over. Although she does not order the scribbles in a developmental sequence, she concludes that these elementary line forms provide the foundation upon which all future artwork is built. Her description of the scribble begins with the dot and then moves to single lines such as vertical, horizontal, diagonal, and curved, followed by multiples of these, and then progresses to roving lines and loops, and culminates with the circle.

In her study of the drawings of 2-year-olds, Kellogg (1970) found that they generally alter the line direction of a scribble, often placing one scribble on top of another. Although they have not developed the skill to draw definitive forms, they do guide their drawing actions so that distinctly suggested shapes are made and then placed on the page with an awareness of the paper edges. By the age of 3, youngsters create diagrams that use single lines to make crosses and to outline triangles and other forms in what Kellogg calls "emergent diagram shapes."

Three- and 4-year-olds normally progress to placing each scribble on a separate page, rather than overlaying them on the same sheet. McCarthy (1924) collected 30,000 children's drawings and concluded that by age 4 youngsters primarily use the outline of a form and combine scribbles more intricately, but do not yet depict mass. It is important to realize that children scribble initially simply for the joy of movement and not because they are interested in representing something or someone.

Symbolism in Drawings

As youngsters approach the age of 4, they begin to attach meaning to their lines. This represents a progression in cognitive development from "kinesthetic thinking to imaginative thinking" (Lowenfeld & Brittain, 1975). While the scribble itself does not objectively look different, there is a major contrast in the child's intent and goals. By this time, children have generally entered Kellogg's (1970) "pictorial" stage, and they represent humans, animals, and other subjects in their drawings. Burt (1921) labels this period "descriptive symbolism," a stage during which parts of the total subject are represented, although with inattention to shape or proportion. In other words, while the youngster may draw a picture of "mommy," mommy's head will be out of proportion to her arms and legs, which at age 5 will typically be presented as short sticks emanating from a round head.

Developing Awareness for Realistic Representations

Beginning at approximately age 7, the youngster becomes increasingly concerned with realistically representing the selected subject. It is at this time that figures are readily recognizable to others and concerns with symmetry, placement, size, use of space, and the creation of an environment for the objects become significant. The typical 7- to 10-year-old will now place a tree in a forest, or next to a house, will include a groundline, and attempt to depict accurate proportions between the tree and the house.

Realistic Portrayals

As children continue to draw and depict objects from their worlds, the ability to represent them more accurately improves. At around age 10, the youngsters become more aware of the various aspects and subtleties of their environments. As such, the drawings will reflect additional details, two- and three-dimensionality, and perspective. Youngsters also may be critical of their own work if it does match their reality perception.

Preadolescent Drawings

Upon entering prepuberty, drawings and doodles begin to express the child's focus on his or her drawings and doodles begin to express the child's focus on his or her emerging sexuality. Prior to this period, sexual differentiation was shown in drawings through clothing, hair styles, and activities. By 11 or 12, normative drawings also add exaggerated sexual characteristics to the human body. A woman may have bulbous breasts or well-rounded buttocks. Another important development of this period is the use of cartoons to voice and camouflage the sexual and identity concerns of this stage.

GENERAL PRINCIPLES IN THE ANALYSIS OF DRAWINGS

When one draws or paints a graphic representation, one's inner world is visually projected for everybody else to view. A child's drawing is an expression and, as such, is a statement that is basically no different from any other statement or sample of behavior. All statements, verbal and nonverbal, including projective drawings, have some meaning for the person who makes them. The challenge for the clinician is to discover the meaning and to find out what the child or adult is trying to communicate through the drawings.

We must emphasize, however, that there is danger in using projective drawing without serious consideration of the artist's age, developmental stage, cognitive strengths, liabilities, and possible neurological impairments. Moreover, while we will shortly review the general areas used in understanding the assertion a drawing makes, we again caution the reader that a drawing or painting must always be assessed within the context of the client's history, behavior, and other evaluative data. "One should bear in mind that most children and adults are not particularly artistically inclined or talented . . . individuals learning to analyze projective drawings are often focused on whether skill or fluency in drawing influence the quality or scope of the interpretive material" (Wohl & Kaufman, 1985, p. 8). The lack of artistic skill does not affect the analysis of the creation, for it is the totality of details that leads us to draw certain hypotheses. In addition, a conclusion should never be drawn based on one drawing. One can be more confident of potential hypotheses by performing a full battery of protective drawings.

Behavioral Observations in Relation to the Drawing Task

The way individuals, particularly children, face paper, pencil, and tester in protective drawing tests provides crucial information about their attitudes and the way in which they relate to the world. The child's interaction with the interviewer and other verbal as well as nonverbal behavior are relevant. As Rubin (1984) notes, "Non-verbally the child speaks just as eloquently. His glance talks, as he looks at the adult for permission, blame, punishment or approval" (p. 67). How the child approaches this new situation will inform us about his or her ability to adjust, handle stress, and master the environment.

The child's silence or verbosity, cheerfulness or dourness, hesitancy or spontaneity, energy and anxiety levels will surface as indicators of his or her more general approach to the world. In addition, if the child generally accepts things in life for the way they are, such as a victimized child who feels powerless and thereby becomes compliant, we may see the youngster use the paper in the position it is given (i.e., vertically). Conversely, if the child has been traumatized and has learned to identify with the aggressor, he or she may turn the page to a horizontal position.

Of course, there are numerous ways to interpret this behavior. These examples are given to highlight the importance of noticing the artist's reaction to the drawing tests. In addition, one should note such behaviors as whether the drawer sets out to draw what is requested or whether the child impulsively scratches it on the paper. Additionally, does the child look pleased with the production upon completion, or dissatisfied and ashamed? Does the child continue with the task, or does the child give up and refuse to continue? It is useful for the therapist to take note of these and other behaviors and expressions, for they will yield rich data when coupled with specific drawing analysis. While the drawings themselves provide us with invaluable information, it would be a great loss to overlook the process through which the individual completes the task.

Decoding the Messages in the Drawing

Just as we form an immediate and overall impression when we first meet a person, so it is when we see a drawing initially. We receive a sense of the artist, for the gestalt of the drawing reflects an aspect(s) of this person's experience with the world. The individual's feelings are projected onto the paper, inviting the viewer to experience them. We may sense sadness, joy, loneliness, agitation, anger, or frivolity, as well as any number of other emotions. The drawing allows us to enter the artist's inner world and, in fact, can even be thought of as a structured interview.

After forming a general impression, we look at more specific aspects of the rendering. While these more formal and quantifiable features provide the guideposts as we systematically chart our way into the artist's world, we caution the reader that they are not laid in concrete and are to be used judiciously. Bear in mind that no single sign can be considered conclusive; rather, it is the totality of symbols that must be assessed.

Placement

Since the placement of the figure or object is less dependent on conscious control than on other features of the drawing, it is a particularly meaningful factor for consideration. The paper serves to mirror the environment, with the placement of the object on the page as a reflection of the child's personality and how the child organizes his or her internal and external world. For example, traumatized children react by becoming overly anxious and may be unable to prevent themselves from scattering objects all over the paper. Conversely, traumatized youngsters who develop obsessive defenses may not be able to refrain from the excruciating and precise placement of each and every line on the page.

A central placement of the drawn work is normal and suggests that the person is reasonably secure (Ogdon, 1977). Hammer (1980) adds that this indicates that the individual is self-directed and self-centered. An image placed above the midline suggests that there are strong strivings towards unrealistic goals. This is particularly relevant when we look at the drawings of sexually abused children whose realities are too painful to face. Youngsters may divert their energies by pushing themselves academically beyond their capacities as a way of refocusing attention away from an untenable family situation. Sexually abused children may alternately overuse fantasy defensively. This might be projected through a high-placed figure or object (Jolles, 1971; Ogdon, 1977). In addition, one's insecurity is reflected by sketching an un-grounded highly placed figure as well as by an image placed well below the midline. A rendering positioned towards the bottom of the page may also be also interpreted as reality-boundedness, concrete thinking, and depression (Hammer, 1980; Jolles, 1964; Ogdon, 1977).

The particular side of the page used may also provide us with information about the creator's own attitudes. Placement on the right side suggests degree of intellectualizing, self-control, and behavior that is environment oriented (Machover, 1980) and strongly regulated by the reality principle (Ogdon, 1977). In addition, this placement may impugn that the person is preoccupied with the future and not focused on the present (Jolles, 1971). Objects located on the left side have been associated with more implulsive individuals and those who are self-absorbed and preoccupied with the past (Jolles, 1971; Ogdon, 1977).

Size

The size of the image presented on the paper is highly significant also (Buck, 1981; Di Leo, 1973; Hammer, 1980; Ogdon, 1977). An average human figure, drawn on a page measuring 8½ by 11 inches by a child of at least 5 years, is generally 9 inches in length (Koppitz, 1968; Ogdon, 1977). Size, like placement, is another factor that is less consciously controlled. The most significant interpretation about size seems to correlate with the artist's self-esteem. If a figure is substantially larger than 9 inches, this might indicate infantile grandi-osity and compensatory defenses (Ogdon, 1977) that are used as a way of camouflaging (even from the artist) deeper feelings of powerlessness and ineffectiveness. Behaviorally, this person is likely to be aggressive and bullying. Conversely, if we are presented with a tiny drawing (one under 2 inches), we may infer that the drawer has strong feelings of inadequacy, inferiority, low self-esteem, and a weak ego (Hammer, 1980; Ogdon, 1977). This individual, whether child or adult, is unable to defend against these feelings as they break through into his or her consciousness, thus creating anxiety and depression.

Details

Detailing, another point examined in the analysis of a drawing, mirrors an individual's awareness and interest in the outside world (Jolles, 1971). Hammer (1980) believes that inadequate detail suggests an inner emptiness, a low energy level, depression, and an introversive type of personality. Ogdon (1977), in his review of the literature, finds that excessive use of detail represents an abnormally strong need to structure the environment. This may be seen in the renderings of sexually abused children whose family life lacks organization and tends to be chaotic. Assessing the details included and/or excluded in a drawing facilitates a better understanding of the conflicts, strengths, and liabilities. The type and number of details that are expected to be present in the drawing, according to established norms, are commensurate with the age of the artist (Harris, 1963; Koppitz, 1968). The normal child will generally include the essential details of the subject and will not add irrelevant items nor delete important ones.

The way in which the details are represented in the rendering, as well as the manner by which they are organized, may be a window into the artist's psyche also. For example, a youngster whose sense of self has become shattered, fragmented, and disorganized in response to sexual traumatization may reflect this state through a disorganized and incoherent theme or by the nonsensical placement of items on the page.

Erasures

Erasures in the production must also be considered in the analysis of the drawing. When used in moderation and followed by an improvement in the drawing, the flexibility and ability to be critical of one's work is reflected (Ogdon, 1977). However, when the erasures result in a deterioration in the quality of the drawing, one should be alert to the probability that a conflictual issue has been tapped. When excessive erasures are present, uncertainty, indecisiveness, and generalized dissatisfaction with one's self are suggested (Hammer, 1980; Koppitz, 1968). This overuse would likely emerge in the drawing of a traumatized youngster since trauma often results in the development of self-distrust and shaken self-esteem.

Line Quality

In a pencil and paper production the quality of the line also needs to be considered. Lines may be drawn faintly, heavily, curved, scribbled, rigidly, or sketchy. The quality of the strokes is reviewed for such factors as firmness, jaggedness, straightness, length, and direction. A firm stroke may indicate that when the artist approaches a task, he or she is determined, persistent, and secure. A curved line may suggest a flexible and healthy personality that is not overly attracted to stereotypical customs (Buck, 1948; Hammer, 1954; Jolles 1964). Lines that appear to have been ruler-drawn perhaps reveal an obsessive-compulsive approach, whereas sketchy lines may show an uncertain, shy, and insecure style. Strokes that are broken or not joined may signify incipient ego disintegration.

The pencil pressure exerted by the artist may be illuminating also. Line pressure may be a gauge of the individual's energy level (Hammer, 1980). When it is fairly consistent throughout the drawn work, it implies normality and stability (Ogdon, 1977). Light pencilling may project a personality colored by hesitation and fearfulness (Di Leo, 1983; Hammer, 1980; Machover, 1980). Heavy strokes suggest inner tension, forcefulness, and a tendency to act aggressively (Hammer, 1980; Ogdon, 1977). In a drawing created by a traumatized youngster we may see areas of pencil pressure so heavy that the paper is torn.

Shading

Another item worth examining is shading. The literature generally agrees that it represents anxiety and/or agitation (Hammer, 1980; Jolles, 1971; Ogdon, 1977). The zone highlighted by shading is most likely symbolic of a conflict area. For example, in the drawing of a house, the chimney is considered a phallic symbol (Jolles, 1971). Children molested by males may shade the chimney, thereby representing their overconcern or preoccupation with the penis.

Transparency

Transparency is another essential point to evaluate in a full drawing analysis. To do so, however, one must be cognizant of its developmental aspect. Although transparencies in drawings are normal for young children, once they are approximately 7 years of age, their presence is either organically or emotionally pathological. Di Leo (1983) correlates Piaget's developmental period of cognition to a parallel advancement in drawing. In the Preoperation Stage, ages 4 to 7, transparencies may be drawn. At this phase in children's lives, they view the world egocentrically and visually reflect this by literally externalizing their internal model onto the paper. Transparencies mirror children's egocentricity and their sense that what they feel and see are experienced by others in exactly the same way at the same moment. Beginning at age 7, according, to Piaget (1962), children enter Concrete Operations. Now they are able to think logically and their drawings will be more realistic. By this phase of development, youngsters are more reality based and know that people cannot see through objects. Therefore the drawings will not have X-ray type of representations. However, where there is an area of anxiety or tension, reality-oriented thinking may break down and a regression to primary-process thinking may ensue. At this point, it may be represented by a transparency. The particular area in which a transparency surfaces flags conflict and/or anxiety.

Symmetry

By age 7, it is normal for children to produce drawings that are symmetric. Asymmetry at this age seems to represent an imbalance associated with poor coordination, impulsivity, organicity, aggression, or inadequate feelings of security (Hammer, 1980; Koppitz, 1968; Ogdon, 1977). Extreme symmetry, on the other hand, is produced most frequently by those individuals who are rigid, emotionally cold, and distant (Ogdon, 1977). This excessive concern with balance is seen most commonly in the drawings of people who tend to be depressed and obsessive-compulsive and are inclined to repress and over-intellectualize.

Projective Drawing Tests

The House-Tree-Person (HTP) Drawing

In 1948, Buck published his early research delineating the House-Tree-Person (HTP) Test. In developing and further refining this test (1947, 1948, 1950, 1951, 1981), he continued to use House, Tree, and Person Drawings because they were familiar to patients of all ages. He also found that clients offered the least resistance to drawing these specific subjects, which are rich with symbolic meaning and stimulate spontaneous discussions. Over time, the drawings of a house, a tree, and a person each created on separate sheets of paper have become meaningful projective tests to help understand the inner structure of an individual. Buck developed an elaborate scoring system to measure both quantitative and qualitative aspects of each drawing. He concluded that using the three drawings concurrently with a client, in one sitting, provided the most reliable interpretative conclusion. Various personality and developmental aspects identified in one drawing could be looked for in the subsequent drawings. Clinical hypotheses could then be confirmed or ruled out by comparative assessments.

The House-Drawing-Test

Webster defines a house as "a permanent dwelling place or living quarters; something that serves for shelter and habitation." The house is the second favorite subject of children to draw (Hammer, 1980). Di Leo (1983) supports this by citing Abbele's (1970) research of drawings by Italian children that showed that houses appeared in 60 percent of the spontaneous drawings created by youngsters between the ages of 6 and 7. Therefore, the request to have a youngster draw a picture of a house is a pleasant, nonthreatening manner in which to gain information.

It is within the house that the basic needs of family life, affection, and security are sought (Di Leo, 1983). Buck (1973) found the House Drawing extremely useful in understanding an individual's inner self. He cataloged essential aspects in this drawing that he believed were normatively present by age 6. He based his inferences on a number of items that he concluded represented intellectual capacities and personality styles. Although he did not offer any substantiating experimental research, he nevertheless presented a variety of assessments, including psychosexual maturity, accessibility, reality testing, interpersonal balance, flexibility of personality, and others. Hammer (1980) concluded that this test is significant in fostering projections since the subject matter reduces the patient's defenses, thereby allowing more material to emerge.

Symbolically, the house serves as a self-portrait, reflecting the artist's body image, maturity, adjustment, accessibility to others, contact with reality, and emotional stability (Buck, 1981; Hammer, 1980). Experts in the field of projective drawings believe that the house also represents children's perception of the parental home. This includes youngsters' views of home life, the quality of their relationship within the family, and their sense of how they are experienced by parents and siblings (Buck, 1981; Di Leo, 1983; Hammer, 1980; Ogdon, 1977).

The viewer's global impression of the house is important in understanding this graphic communication. This translates into experiencing the house and its surroundings as a whole, without regard to details. Is the house a pleasant place, or is it frightening? Is it welcoming or foreboding? Is this a home you would want to go into, or stay away from?

After this initial sense, specific factors such as size, placement, line quality, line pressure, dimensionality, perspective, the presence of transparencies, and the inclusion of essential, nonessential, and bizarre details are all examined. It is expected by the time the artist is 6 years old that the house will contain at least one door, one window, one wall, a roof, and a chimney (Buck, 1981). How each of these items is represented has symbolic meaning. In addition, when interpreting the House Drawing the clinician should note which rooms are included or excluded, the presence or absence of pathway(s), the use of entrance details, and the inclusion or exclusion of a groundline.

The door of a house is considered a representation of the youngster's accessibility (Jolles, 1964). An open door may be suggestive of a strong need for emotional warmth and connotes the potential vulnerability of a person who goes to extreme levels to satisfy this craving. This drawn symbol is comparable to leaving the door of one's house wide open for there is as implicit invitation for anyone to enter without the host having the capability to screen out hostile and dangerous guests. The drawing of a house that contains no door reflects the artist's tendency to withdraw from the environment by blocking contact with others.

Windows, adequate in number and size, indicate normal personal accessibility (Hammer, 1980). The absence of windows is the child's way of saying, "I'll make it impossible for you to see in." At the same time, the youngster pays a price for he or she cannot see out. In understanding the symbolism communicated by the door and the windows, it is important to look at the location, number, style, size, proportions, emphasis, and details. Often a person with secrets to hide will put all the windows above ground level or shade the ground floor window to prevent others from seeing within. At all costs the secrets must be preserved. One of the ways sexually abused children may try to cope with the effects of the abuse is to isolate themselves and withdraw from interpersonal contact. This would be reflected in a house that contains no door or windows such as that seen in Plate 1 drawn by 7-year-old, sexually abused Gail.

Walls generally connote ego strength; strong walls are equated with a sturdy ego and thin walls with a fragile one. Overemphasized walls are attributed to the artist's strong and conscious need to main ego control (Jolles, 1964). The chimney represents both a phallus and a symbol of warmth in the youngster's close relationships. The particular treatment given to this part of the house, such as its emphasis, reinforcement, absence, size, and the number are all significant. The characteristics of the chimney smoke, including its presence or absence, direction, shape, and intensity, must also be considered.

Buck (1981) states that there is sound empirical evidence for the assumption that the roof signifies thinking and fantasy when the house is viewed as a psychological self-portrait. The relative size of the roof, in proportion to the rest of the building, tends to indicate the amount of time and energy devoted to fantasy. Overemphasis of the roof is most often seen in drawings by people who are afraid of losing control over fantasy life. Miriam, age 5, an unfortunate victim of sexual assault, demonstrates this in her drawing of a house in which the brickwork or shingling draws our attention to the roof (Plate 2). Conversely, the omission of a roof, or one depicted by only a single line, reflects an inability to daydream—to fantasize in other ways (Hammer, 1980).

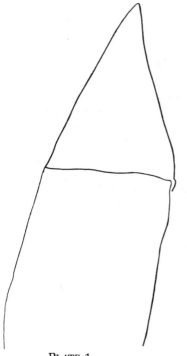

PLATE 1.

PLATE 2.

An important component of the analysis of the House Drawing is the Post-Drawing interview. (PDI). Jolles, Buck, Hammer and others suggested questions that enhance and expand upon the database. The questions that we find most helpful are: Where is this house? How old is it? Is that young or old in house terms? What is its best part? What is its worst part? What does this house need the most? We also find that asking the artist to tell a story about the house is often a relatively painless way in which to enrich the information base.

The Tree-Test

Trees are referred to throughout classical literature, mythology, poetry, and children's stories. As such, the tree is endowed with rich symbolic meaning. It has represented life and growth from earliest recorded times. Jucker (1928, cited by Koch, 1952), a vocational consultant, was the first clinician to become interested in the drawing of a tree and its possible relevance for aptitude testing. Koch (1952) built on this early work and developed an organized system to interpret this rendering. He considered the Tree Drawing as an illustration of the essence of the person who drew it.

Koch (1952) concluded that the Tree Drawing reveals an externalization of that which is within—a blend of deep-seated and surface layers of the self represented on paper. Hammer (1980), who believes that a Tree Drawing represents a projection of the deepest levels of the personality, stated that it is a symbol reflecting the hidden affects in relation to the self and tapping the most primitive part of one's personality. Additionally, he posits that object relations and relatedness are also projected onto the tree, which represent the person in relation to his milieu. The tree, as a natural and vegetative form, draws upon fundamental and enduring feelings in relation to the self and, of all the drawings, it is less likely to change over time.

Because of its significance as a projective tool, the tree must first be viewed globally. What kind of a tree is drawn? A fruit tree created by someone over age 7 depicts possible immaturity, although it is normal for child between 5 and 7 (Koch, 1952). A Christmas tree flags dependency needs; dead trees are drawn by extremely depressed individuals with profound feelings of inferiority and potential suicidal behavior (Hammer, 1968). The size of the tree is also telling. Hugo, a 6-year-old boy, was sexually exploited. In his drawing of a tree (Plate 3), we see a huge tree which indicates possible aggressive tendencies, fantasy, or hypersensitivity (Buck, 1948, 1950).

The tree is comprised of essential details including roots, a trunk, branches, and a crown. By the age of 7 we expect the inclusion of the trunk and at least one branch (Buck, 1981). In contrast to other drawings, the tree is less subject to developmental variations after this age (Koch, 1952). However, even in the presentation of these two primary components, there is infinite variation in the manner in which they are presented. It is these differences that provide valuable clues about the inner workings of the artist.

Each detail about the tree carries a distinct meaning. The clinician is interested in examining where the tree is set on the paper, the presentation of its outline, the texture of the trunk, and any fluctuations in its width (Koch, 1952). Children 8 years or younger would be expected to place the tree on the

PLATE 3.

bottom edge of the paper ("paper-based"). However, when this is executed by an individual above age 10, it depicts immaturity and a certain narrowness in viewing the world. The trunk embodies feelings of basic power, ego intactness, and inner strength (Buck, 1981) and can be compared to the torso in the Human Figure Drawing. A dashed line in the outline of a trunk may delineate anxiety, impulsivity, or affective lability. Scars or holes symbolize feelings of damage, and when placed at a particular point in the trunk, scars or holes mirror the age at which the trauma was experienced (Lyons, 1955). The base of the tree is viewed as the beginning of life, with the top of the trunk representing the artist's current age.

The branches of a tree literally extend into the surroundings. Their number, size, dimensionality, and the extent of their structure is the metaphoric embodiment of our personality organization and of our interaction with the world. A well-organized branch structure along with well-formed branches suggest normal flexibility and satisfactory adjustment (Ogdon, 1977). Branches that are directed towards the center of the tree or that are arched inward connote a sense of independence and a possible withdrawal from others. Bare branches that are one-dimensional and fan-shaped intimate impulsivity, arrogance, and instability (Koch, 1952). The possible loss of one's ability to cope with environmental pressures may be signaled by falling branches (Buck, 1981).

The roots, which should not be visible to the observer, are the symbolic indices of personality stability. Koch (1952) states that the tree lives in two directions; there is growth both upward and downward. The function of the roots is to feed the tree sustenance from the earth and to provide stability by clinging to the earth. Just as the tree needs to be rooted to live and grow, a person likewise needs to feel securely grounded. The basic stability of a sexually abused youngster, whose security has been shaken by the assaulted might, therefore, be reflected in a tree drawn without even a suggestion of rootedness. For the child more seriously affected by such abuse, we might see exposed roots, which are in effect transparencies that illustrate poor ties to reality.

Similar to the House-Drawing-Test, The Tree-Test yields the most information when interpreted in conjunction with a Post-Drawing Interview. This process enables the artist to further define, describe, embellish, or even modify his or her work. We have used the following questions: What kind of tree is this? What is its best part? What is its worst part? Is it alive or dead? Is it alone or with other trees? Does it have seeds? What does it need the most? Tell a story about the tree.

The Human Figure Drawing (HFD)

Of all the types of drawings created by children, the human figure is the favorite subject (Griffith, 1935) and seems to embody children's feelings about themselves. According to Hammer (1980), drawing a person can elicit a person's affect in relation to the self, the ideal self, and perceptions of significant others. In addition, personality traits, attitudes, concerns, and interpersonal skills are depicted. Koppitz (1968) states that the pictorial response to the task of creating an HFD represents a graphic form of communication between the child and the therapist, and, as such, differs from spontaneous renderings that the child may make when alone or with friends.

When analyzing the HFD, the examiner/therapist studies the drawing, taking note of size, placement, line quality, shading, erasures, transparencies, emotions elicited, and general themes. Attention is given to the inclusion and exclusion of details that would normatively be present at specific ages. Each part of the body holds meaning and becomes a symbolic projection of various aspects of the self. Developmentally, the human face is the first thing to which a child responds. The face is the area through which social contact is made and satisfaction obtained. By observing facial expressions, children soon learn what they can anticipate. It is not surprising that young children concentrate on the head and face and little else. The head is the location of thoughts, fantasy life, and the center for intellectual power. It is also the seat for control of bodily impulses. Older children, or adults, who have been sexually abused may focus on the head in the drawing of a person. This suggests a method for coping with abuse that involves an overemphasis on thought and a possible denial of feelings and bodily urges.

The torso and body is identified with drives; shoulders characteristically represent one's ability to shoulder or handle life. Arms and hands mirror interpersonal relations and the individual's capacity to make contact with the environment. Legs and feet depict feelings of groundedness and mobility. Head, body, and legs are generally present on the HFDs of children by age 5; other items such as arms, shoulders, pupils, mouth, and fingers continue to increase in frequency of occurrence from ages 5 to 12. Significantly, research reveals that the frequency of occurrence of most of these items is not affected by a youngster's drawing ability. For example, by age 6 for girls and 10 for boys, regardless of drawing skills, we anticipate the presence of a neck (Koppitz, 1968). The neck connects the head and body and signifies the modulation between thoughts and drives. The absence of this body part by a child significantly older than this normative age, or conversely its presence in the drawing by a much younger child, alerts us to the possibility that the youngster may be having difficulty with bodily impulses and concerns. On Plate 4 we see an elongated neck drawn by 5-year-old Ray, who was a victim of his father's sexual attack. This child manifested a host of disturbances, which included placing himself in dangerous situations and even engaging in self-injurious acts.

The presence of extraneous details, such as clouds, alerts us to possible depression and anxiety, symptoms familiar to sexually abused children. Shading in a specific body area reveals anxiety in relation to the symbolic meaning attached to that part. Heavily shaded hair may suggest oversexualization (Urban, 1963), which results in feelings of agitation. Both of these representations are present in 7-year-old Mack's drawing of a person. This boy was periodically sexually abused by his paternal uncle over a span of several years (Plate 5).

PLATE 4.

PLATE 5.

The above factors are used in the qualitative analysis of drawings. Koppitz (1968) was interested in studying drawings quantitatively as well. She researched and identified a list of 30 indicators, reflected in the Human Figure Drawings of children ages 5 to 12, which she believed signified potential emotional disturbances. She emphasizes that a number of these items must be present to signal the likelihood of problems. These indicators include three categories of items. The first is scored in regard to the quality of the drawing and includes such aspects as poor integration of parts of the figure; shading of the face or any part of it; shading of the body and/or limbs, hands and/or neck; gross asymmetry of limbs; tiny figures (less than 2''); and enlarged figures (more than 9''). The second category consists of items not typical to the HFD, such as crossed eyes; teeth; arms too short to reach waistline; arms that reach below the knees; hands as big as the face; arms without hands or fingers; genitals; legs pressed together; and the presence of rain or snow. The following omissions comprise the third category of items included in Koppitz's list of potential emotional indicators: eyes, nose, mouth, body, and arms (should be included once boys are 6 and girls are 5); feet (expected from boys by age 9 and girls by age 7); and hair (expected to be present in boys' HFDs by age 10 and in girls' HFDs by age 6).

In addition to looking at both the qualitative and quantitative aspects of the HFD, it is important to include a Post-Drawing Interview. Among the questions we find useful are: How old is this person? What is his/her best part? What is his/her worst part? What does he/she need the most? Tell a story about this person.

Kinetic Family Drawing (KFD)

Just as Gestalt psychologists conclude that the whole is greater than the sum of its parts, the family as an interactive system is more powerful than the total of the individual members. The family is a dynamic force that influences the growth and development of the offspring and even the continued evolution of the parents. In the process of growing, identification of the child's self emerges through the internalization of the parental figures' feelings and values. If these are positive and growth-enhancing, the offspring will likely develop healthy and positive self-concepts. If these feelings and values are negative, the youngsters may develop negative self-concepts. To adequately understand the child, the family's history, dynamics, and value structure mandate attention.

When a child is told "Draw your family doing something together" (Kinetic Family Drawing), the child's subjective family experience is graphically presented. Burns and Kaufman (1972) espouse that the KFD is a statement of how the child perceives him or herself in the family setting and how the youngster views the interactions between family members. Historically, children were simply asked to create a drawing of their family as part of a battery of projective tests. Burns and Kaufman, after two decades of testing in this format, expanded the technique by requesting that the artist draw his or her family "doing something." They hypothesized that this additional information would shed light on the child's object relations.

In interpreting children's KFDs, specific points should be noted. As in the production of the Human Figure Drawing, each person represented is individually evaluated. It is important to be aware of how each family member in the KFD is using his or her body. Is it being used exhibitionistically, to hide, or to be seductive? Does the individual appear proud or ashamed? The manner in which each person is drawn symbolizes how that family member is perceived by the child.

Minuchin (1981), in his theory of structural family therapy, addresses the issues of boundaries between parents and children. The parents should be a separate entity with explicit roles of power and dominance. When the family system has broken down, a child may assume the responsibility or role of a parent. The role that each family member plays may be depicted graphically in the KFD through size, position, and placement. If one child has become parentified, as often happens in the incestuous family, we might see this person drawn larger than siblings or even the adults (Plate 6). The parentified child may hold a position of dominance on the page, such as in the middle, around which all activity centers, or may be placed high on the page looking down on other family members. We also gain information in regard to the child's role through the activity in which he or she is engaged. Is the child cooking dinner for the parent, or performing another action representing over-responsibility? In other words, who is dependent on whom—often a confused position in incestuous families—is graphically presented for the viewer.

There is a continuum along which individuals differentiate from their families (Bowen, 1978). This theoretical line begins with total dependency and ends with total differentiation. A healthy person develops somewhere along the midpoint. When family members are fused and there is little sense of individuation, as in the sexually abusive family, there is concern for the health of the system. This enmeshment, which typifies the separation anxiety often present in the incestuous family, may be reflected in the drawing by the figures' stereotypic similarities. Are the figures all the same height regardless of ages? Are they wearing the same clothes? Are they all in the same position or

PLATE 6.

Church

Brother   Mother   Father   Me

PLATE 7.

stance? With the exception of the portrayal of the artist, we see this represented in 9-year-old Ellen's drawing of her family in church (Plate 7). It is critical to realize that some likenesses are to be expected since there must be identifications in any family. However, some sense of separateness or uniqueness must also exist in a functional unit. We might see this differentiation by posture, action, or dress.

Family coalitions, alliances, and disharmonies are other dynamics revealed through a study of the KFD. In the incestuous family, where collusion is always present to some extent, this might be portrayed by compartmentalization. The isolation a daughter feels from her mother, due to incest, may well be mirrored in the child's drawing, by her positioning of herself further away from her mother than from other family members. Generally, intimacy and estrangement are shown in KFDs by the closeness and distance of the members from each other as well as in the implied or rendered action. Are they engaged in a cooperative activity with everyone involved? Or are they all off doing their own thing?

Other factors to consider in analyzing the KFD are omission or inclusion of members, including the artist, as well as erasures, shading, transparencies, and line quality. In addition the Post-Drawing Interview should include such questions as: Tell me who each person is and how old is he or she? Who is happiest? Why? Who is saddest? Why? Tell me what the family is doing.

THE APPLICATION OF PROJECTIVE DRAWINGS WITH SEXUALLY ABUSED CHILDREN

A difficulty presented to professionals is how to assess and diagnose sexual abuse. Cases with clear medical evidence constitute only about 10 percent of the abusive situations. Adult witnesses to corroborate the sexual attack are equally rare. It therefore becomes the responsibility of the clinical community to properly identify cases of sexual abuse. However, this is an arduous task since children are often reticent to disclose or confirm information regarding the allegations.

Experts (Finkelhor & Browne, 1985; Sgroi, 1982; Summit & Kryso, 1978) have noted that the disclosure of sexual violations is a complex situation complicated by many issues. The child frequently has a relationship with the perpetrator (Finkelhor & Browne, 1985), which brings to the forefront such profound issues as loyalty and the fear of losing this significant person once the abuse is revealed. In addition, when the sexual abuse involves more of a "seduction" than a "rape," the child often receives gratification through this special, albeit pathological, union. There may also be ambivalent feelings towards the abuser and about the act itself, both of which tend to motivate the child to remain silent.

Family members are frequently not receptive to accepting the reality of the abuse and may place overt and covert pressures on the child to "keep the secret" in face of possible resultant financial, social, and familial disintegration. Additionally, the child may fear being blamed for the victimization. Even when youngsters, despite all these pressures, have been able to tell about the abuses, there is often a need for more "objective" evidence, since children's statements are generally viewed with suspicion.

Current literature substantiates the use and viability of drawings with sexually abused youngsters. Kelley (1984, 1985) notes that children do not possess an adult vocabulary. Drawings, therefore, become an excellent tool through which they are able to communicate. Kelley identified unique aspects of the Human Figure Drawings created by molested youngsters, which include such items as a figure sketched with broken lines; shaded genitals and chests; clown figures; omission of arms; and mouth emphasis. Cohen and Phelps (1985), investigating whether incestuously abused children's drawings yielded markers flagging suspicions of sexual abuse, developed 12 indices of molestation. These consisted of the presence of any of the following: a red house; only one window in a house; a phallic tree; a phallic chimney; a colored-in face; an enclosed person; violent content; and the absence of color when a variety of colors are offered.

Hibbard, Roghmann, and Hoekelman (1987) researched the presence of sexual parts in pictures pencilled by the sexually misused child. Although they found no significant differences in their drawings as compared to control groups, they found that sexual derivatives, rather than the direct representation of sexual parts, are generally present in the drawings of sexually abused youngsters.

PILOT STUDY OF PROJECTIVE DRAWINGS TO SUGGEST SEXUAL ABUSE

Because of the difficulties often encountered in having objective proof of sexual abuse through such accepted means as confession, medical evidence or the testimony of witnesses, the authors developed a pilot research project to further ascertain whether projective drawings could provide objective indices of sexual abuse. Browne and Finkelhor's (1986) conceptual framework, "The Traumagenic Dynamics of the Impact of Child Sexual Abuse," provided the theoretical basis for the project. As discussed earlier, Finkelhor and Browne conclude that the effects of sexual abuse are manifested in four areas: traumatic sexualization; stigmatization; betrayal; and powerlessness. They have additionally identified the psychological impact and behavioral manifestation for each sphere.

In developing the protocol for the pilot, the authors identified drawing items found in the House, Tree, Person, and Kinetic Family Drawings that correlate with the specific psychological impacts and behaviors that Browne and Finkelhor (1986) recognized in their conceptual framework. Since child-victims of sexual abuse suffer from the impacts identified by Browne and Finkelhor, and since projective drawing markers are recognized as reflecting the conscious and unconscious dynamics, actions, and feelings of the artists, it was hypothesized that items specifically correlated to the model would be present in sexually abused youngsters' drawings. A listing of such details was assembled from acknowledged researchers and authors on projective drawings including Buck (1973); Hammer (1980); Jolles (1971); Koch (1952); Koppitz (1968); and Ogdon (1977). A total of 86 items were included in the comparative analysis of hypothesized indices projecting sexual abuse; 24 in the area of betrayal; 32 in traumatic sexualization; 19 in stigmatization; and 11 in powerlessness.

The subjects of this pilot study consisted of 18 children known to mental health services who had no history of sexual abuse, 18 children drawn randomly from the community, and 18 child-victims of sexual abuse. A victim of sexual abuse had to have been abused within the past six months. Additionally, the abuse had to have been validated either by a witness, medical evidence, or confession of the perpetrator. All of the children involved in the research were between the ages of 5 and 10 years. The median ages of the children were as follows: sexually abused girls—7.6 years; sexually abused boys—6.15 years; sexually abused children—6.88 years; clinic girls—8.1 years; clinic boys—7.5 years; clinic children—7.93 years; random girls—5.8 years; random boys—6.6 years; random children—6.55 years.

The analysis of the pictures drawn by the 54 children included in this pilot study clearly indicates the necessity for continued research. The results also indicate that the Kinetic Family Drawing has very great potential as an investigative tool. The four elements of betrayal, traumatic sexualization, stigmatization, and powerlessness were assessed in the House, Tree, and Person Drawings. Only three of the four, traumatic sexualization, powerlessness, and stigmatization, can be assessed in the KFD.

Tables 1 and 2 present the results for males and females and for the age groups 4 to 6 and 7 to 10. The age-related material does not include the clinic group, as 15 of the 16 children fell into the 7- to 10-year-old category. The mean ages for three groups were 6.5 years for the abused and the control groups and 8.1 years for the clinic group.

The three groups—the abused children, the clinic children, and the control group—were differentiated in these ANOVA tests. Abused boys and girls were identifiable ($p < .01$) using the Kinetic Family Drawing. With less accuracy, abused girls could be identified using the Person Drawing and abused boys using the Tree Drawing. The latter may be clinically valid when we understand that the tree, as a growing vegetative form, may at some level relate to the "growing" shape of the erect penis and that the injury to a male's sense of his virility may be unconsciously connected to the tree.

As in Table 1, the KFD permitted the identification of the abused group ($p < .05$ for 4- to 6-year-olds and $p < .01$ for 7- to 10-year-olds). The Tree portion of the House-Tree-Person Test was a powerful measure in the younger group, more so than the KFD. This may conceivably be a result of the different drawing and cognitive skills reflected in the two instruments (i.e., the concept of inclusion and exclusion may, in fact, become more pronounced in the older child).

Chi-square analyses were performed for the elements of betrayal (Table 3), traumatic sexualization (Table 4), stigmatization (Table 5), and powerlessness (Table 6). There were statistically significant results in all four investigations. For items representing betrayal, significant group difference was found in the Person Drawing. Among the three groups, the abused group was found to have

TABLE 1
Group Differences for Males and Females

Gender	Topic	Abused Mean	(N)	Clinic Mean	(N)	Control Mean	(N)
				GROUP			
Female	House	4.63	(8)	4.89	(9)	4.70	(10)
	Tree	2.88	(8)	4.33	(9)	3.60	(10)
	Person[+]	6.63	(8)	3.44	(9)	4.40	(10)
	KFD**	2.75	(8)	2.00	(9)	0.70	(10)
SUBTOTAL		4.22	(32)	3.67	(36)	3.35	(40)
Male	House	4.57	(7)	5.57	(7)	5.00	(6)
	Tree*	2.25	(8)	4.00	(7)	3.33	(6)
	Person	7.00	(8)	4.29	(7)	6.33	(6)
	KFD**	3.25	(8)	1.29	(7)	1.33	(6)
SUBTOTAL		4.26	(31)	3.79	(28)	4.00	(24)
All	House	4.60	(15)	5.19	(16)	4.81	(16)
	Tree**	2.56	(16)	4.19	(16)	3.50	(16)
	Person**	6.81	(16)	3.81	(16)	5.13	(16)
	KFD**	3.00	(16)	1.69	(16)	0.93	(16)
TOTAL		4.24	(63)	3.72	(64)	3.59	(16)

[+]p<.10 LEVEL
*p<.05 LEVEL
**p<.01 LEVEL

TABLE 2
Group Differences for Younger and Older Children

Age	Topic	Abused Mean	(N)	Control Mean	(N)
4- to 6-year-olds	House	4.86	(7)	4.71	(7)
	Tree**	2.00	(8)	4.29	(7)
	Person	8.25	(8)	5.57	(7)
	KFD*	3.25	(8)	1.29	(7)
SUBTOTAL		4.58	(31)	3.96	(28)
7- to 10-year-olds	House	4.38	(8)	4.89	(9)
	Tree	3.13	(8)	2.89	(9)
	Person	5.38	(8)	4.78	(9)
	KFD**	2.75	(8)	0.67	(9)
SUBTOTAL		3.91	(32)	3.31	(36)
All	House	4.60	(15)	4.81	(16)
	Tree*	2.56	(16)	3.50	(16)
	Person	6.81	(16)	5.13	(16)
	KFD**	3.00	(16)	0.93	(16)
TOTAL		4.24	(63)	3.59	(64)

Note: The clinic group was not included in this comparison because 15 out of the 16 children belong to the older age group.
*p<.05 LEVEL
**p<.01 LEVEL

TABLE 3
Betrayal

	Abused Freq.	Pct.	Clinic Freq.	Pct.	Control Freq.	Pct.	Total Freq.	Pct.	X^2
Total items present	52	(25.0%)	51	(24.5%)	48	(23.1%)	151	(24.2%)	.23
HOUSE									
Total items absent	156	(75.0%)	157	(75.5%)	160	(76.9%)	473	(75.8%)	
Total items present	26	(18.1%)	28	(19.4%)	29	(20.1%)	83	(19.2%)	.21
TREE									
Total items absent	118	(81.9%)	116	(80.6%)	115	(79.9%)	349	(80.8%)	
Total items present	10	(15.6%)	1	(1.6%)	4	(6.3%)	15	(7.8%)	9.11
PERSON									
Total items absent	54	(84.4%)	63	(98.4%)	60	(93.7%)	177	(92.2%)	
Total items present	88	(21.2%)	80	(19.2%)	81	(19.5%)	249	(20.0%)	.57
TOTAL									
Total items absent	328	(78.8%)	336	(80.8%)	335	(80.5%)	999	(80.0%)	
@ p<.05									

TABLE 4
Traumatic Sexualization

	Abused		Clinic		Control		Total		X^2
	Freq.	Pct.	Freq.	Pct.	Freq.	Pct.	Freq.	Pct.	
Total items present	19	(19.8%)	28	(29.2%)	23	(24.7%)	70	(24.3%)	2.3
HOUSE									
Total items absent	77	(80.2%)	68	(70.8%)	73	(75.3%)	218	(75.7%)	
Total items present	12	(18.8%)	12	(18.8%)	11	(17.2%)	35	(18.2%)	.07
TREE									
Total items absent	52	(81.2%)	52	(81.2%)	53	(82.8%)	157	(21.8%)	
Total items present	53	(16.6%)	41	(12.8%)	32	(10.0%)	126	(13.1%)	6.1 @
PERSON									
Total items absent	267	(83.4%)	279	(87.2%)	288	(90.0%)	834	(86.9%)	
Total items present	4	(8.3%)	4	(8.3%)	0	(0.0%)	8	(5.6%)	4.2
KFD									
Total items absent	44	(91.7%)	44	(91.7%)	48	(100.0%)	136	(94.4%)	
Total items present	88	(16.7%)	85	(16.1%)	66	(12.5%)	239	(15.1%)	4.2
TOTAL									
Total items absent	440	(83.3%)	443	(83.9%)	462	(87.5%)	1345	(84.9%)	

@ p<.05

TABLE 5
Stigmatization

	Abused		Clinic		Control		Total		X^2
	Freq.	Pct.	Freq.	Pct.	Freq.	Pct.	Freq.	Pct.	
Total items present	17	(21.3%)	22	(27.5%)	18	(22.5%)	57	(23.8%)	0.97
HOUSE									
Total items absent	63	(78.7%)	58	(72.5%)	62	(77.5%)	183	(76.2%)	
Total items present	20	(20.8%)	33	(34.4%)	24	(25.0%)	77	(26.7%)	4.72
TREE									
Total items absent	76	(79.2%)	63	(65.6%)	72	(75.0%)	211	(73.3%)	
Total items present	10	(10.4%)	4	(4.2%)	9	(9.4%)	23	(8.0%)	2.93
PERSON									
Total items absent	86	(89.6%)	92	(95.8%)	87	(90.6%)	265	(92.0%)	
Total items present	21	(32.8%)*	8	(12.5%)	2	(3.1%)	31	(16.1%)	21.77 @
KFD									
Total items absent	43	(67.2%)	56	(87.5%)	62	(96.9%)	161	(83.9%)	
Total items present	68	(20.2%)	67	(19.9%)	53	(15.8%)	188	(18.7%)	2.76
TOTAL									
Total items absent	268	(79.8%)	269	(80.1%)	283	(84.2%)	820	(81.3%)	

@ p<.0001

TABLE 6
Powerlessness

	Abused		Clinic		Control		Total		
	Freq.	Pct.	Freq.	Pct.	Freq.	Pct.	Freq.	Pct.	X^2
Total items present	2	(12.5%)	1	(6.3%)	3	(18.8%)	6	(12.5%)	1.44
HOUSE									
Total items absent	14	(87.5%)	15	(93.7%)	13	(81.2%)	42	(87.5%)	
Total items present	1	(6.3%)	0	(0.0%)	0	(0.0%)	1	(2.1%)	2.04
TREE									
Total items absent	15	(93.7%)	16	(100.0%)	16	(100.0%)	47	(97.9%)	
Total items present	31	(21.5%)	14	(9.7%)	21	(14.6%)	66	(15.3%)	7.83
PERSON									
Total items absent	113	(78.5%)	130	(90.3%)	123	(85.4%)	366	(84.7%)	
Total items present	34	(19.3%)	15	(8.5%)	24	(13.6%)	73	(13.8%)	8.62
TOTAL									
Total items absent	142	(80.7%)	161	(91.5%)	152	(86.4%)	455	(86.2%)	
@ p<.05									

the highest number of betrayal items embedded in their drawings of a person ($p < .05$). The most common, and different item, was the presence of clouds in the Person Drawings of the abused group. Neither of the other two clusters had clouds in their drawings. Traumatic Sexualization items were also evident more often in the Person Drawing ($p < .05$). Among the drawing details significant to this sequelae, the open mouth, long hair, and hair thinning at the crown were more common in the group of abused youngsters.

Items embedded in the Kinetic Family Drawings related to stigmatization were significantly more evident in the drawings of the abused children as well ($p < .0001$). We conjecture that this high level of statistical significance can be attributed to the level of guilt and shame sexually abused children feel and how different they see themselves from other family members. Powerlessness items were also notably different from group to group ($p < .05$) in the Person Drawings of the three groups. Items found more often among the abused were, again, open mouth and the clouds.

In summation, the following items were found to be significant ($p < .01$) using the ANOVA for both sexually abused boys and girls in the Kinetic Family, Tree, and Person Drawings. In the KFD: the presence of the penis, compartmentalization, and boxlike figures, and the artist depicted significantly different from other family members. In the Tree Drawings: separation of the trunk from the crown, the absence of any keyhole trees (other groups had significant numbers thus depicted), dead trees, and the absence of leaves. In the Person Drawings: the presence of teeth, large noses (larger than one-third of face), open mouths, bald heads, hair thinning at the crown, long hair (past the shoulders), monster-like figures, transparencies at the genital area, and the presence of clouds.

These results are presented to demonstrate the need for additional research in this area. It is the authors' hypothesis that the use of Kinetic Family Drawings and House-Tree-Person instruments, in concert with Browne and Finkelhor's construct of the Traumagenic Dynamics of Child Sexual Abuse, may well prove to be a reliable mechanism by which the probability of sexual abuse can, in the very least, be flagged, if not identified.

CHAPTER 3

THE PROJECTIONS OF EGO FUNCTIONS OF SEXUALLY ABUSED CHILDREN

Most theorists and clinicians agree on the importance of the latency stage of development, although they differ in their perception of "the work of latency" (Sarnoff, 1976). Latency is a time when multiple phenomena are occurring simultaneously. Intrapsychic structures are being solidified and the personality organization takes foothold. Within the character, ethical and moral standards are established and characteristic defense mechanisms are developed. Most important, the youngster evolves the use of fantasy as a means to control and limit his or her sexual and aggressive drives. Fantasy enables repression and thereby becomes an essential tool for the child to channel aggressive and sexual impulses into productive activities.

The ability to complete tasks, problem solve, plan, see cause and effect relationships, and learn academic and social skills occur during this period also. The parallel play of earlier childhood changes into the ability to use peers as helpmates. The use of toys evolves from seeking comfort to facilitating fantasy development and ego enhancement. At the same time, the cathexis of the child shifts from the family to the parental introject, enabling the youngster to begin to relate to the larger society. As the child interacts more actively with those outside the home, he or she has an opportunity to compare and contrast her or himself with others. The child's comparable success at school and the ability to develop positive relationships strongly influence his or her evolving sense of self and measure of self-worth.

Not surprisingly, for the child-victim of sexual molestation, latency development becomes troublesome. Experiencing a mature sexual experience interferes with and negatively affects a youngster's normal development either at the time of occurrence, immediately after disclosure, and/or in the future. Finkelhor (1986), after surveying current research and carefully analyzing the statistics generated, concludes that there is a surge in the vulnerability of children for sexual abuse at ages 6 and 7 and a subsequent rise again at age 10. As such, in addition to all the growth-producing experiences the period of latency affords youngsters, it is also the predominant stage at which sexual abuse takes place.

Moreover, ongoing developmental advances are severely impeded when, through sexual abuse, the oedipal wishes become realities, for it is the very inhibition of the oedipal desires, and the concomitant frustration, which push the child to the next phase. However, when a sexual relationship exists, particularly between a parent and a youngster, the child's age-appropriate involvement with others, such as peers and teachers, becomes constricted. Instead, the child becomes even more tied to the parental figure with whom he or she develops a private repertoire of memories and satisfactions. Anna Freud (1982) maintains that

> normal development presupposes that the oedipal phantasies remain just as they are, namely irrealities. It is their frustration which leads to the overcoming of the Oedipus complex, which initiates entrance into the latency period with its inestimable benefits for ego advancement, super-ego formation and personality development. (p. 34)

ALTERATIONS IN EGO FUNCTIONS

Organization of Defenses

One of the major tasks of latency is the organization and solidification of the child's defenses. The defense mechanisms protect the ego against overwhelming anxiety and painful affects. Without adequate defenses, this anxiety and its concomitant feelings have the potential to cause impairment to the ego. The ego, as the apparatus responsible for carrying out vital and organizing tasks, assures the continuity of a child's psychological evolution. When a youngster is assaulted by sexual trauma, there is the potential that his or her ego could be seriously debilitated.

Williams (1987) notes that sexual molestation can cause the instincts to become diffused and disordered, leading to a state in which impulses run amuck. This interrupts ego development and leads to fixation at early developmental levels.

> When repudiating the claims of instinct, its [the ego] first task must always be to come to terms with . . . affects. Love, longing, jealousy, mortification, pain, and mourning accompany sexual wishes; hatred, anger, and rage accompany the impulses of aggression; if the instinctual demands with which they are associated are to be warded off, these affects must submit to all the various measures to which the ego resorts in its efforts to master them. (A. Freud, (1966, p. 32)

MASTERING OF AFFECTS

The capacity of a sexually molested child to master the feelings that abuse engenders is quite limited by virtue of their overwhelming strength. For the abused child-victim—especially of incest—love, and particularly parental love, takes on a new and confusingly perverse dimension. The incestuously abused child who becomes the oedipal victor develops a exaggerated sense of jealousy, simultaneously hating and desiring both parents, as well as fearing that both or either may be taken from him or her. Such youngsters live on the precipice of abandonment, dreading an intense loss at any moment. Over time, the child's attempts to cope with the flooding of these extreme emotions may culminate in emotional numbing or psychological deadness.

The cost of such defensive blocking may result in feelings of helplessness which, in turn, evolve into passivity. This is especially significant for the young latency-age child for whom the developmental task of initiating activity is paramount and synonymous with the satisfaction experienced in attacking a job and victoriously mastering it. The normal stamina used for these ends, generally accessible to the latency-age child, may be noticeably absent for the sexually abused youngster. This victim's energy is instead consumed with issues of safety, abandonment, freedom from physical harm, and torn loyalties. As a result, the child is often unable to pursue activities throuigh which he or she learns to master environmental challenges. Since the self-assertions of the sexually molested child are often thwarted by the abuser, the youngster's ability to self-direct is hampered. This frequently leads to guilt and a lack of joy associated with acquiring new skills. As the ability to acquire new skills within a social peer context becomes primary for the older latency-age child, the consequences of not being able to achieve this creates a strong sense of inferiority within the child.

Additionally, the molested latency child is faced not only with normal developmental demands, but also with pressures to fulfill the perpetrator's sexual and emotional needs. This is clearly overtaxing to the child's limited resources and often contributes to the unsuccessful resolution of latency. The violated youngster may be unable to establish an adequate foundation on which to develop the fundamental tools of responsible living which allow him or her to find a task intrinsically satisfying. If this satisfaction is absent, it adds to the child's difficulties in identifying with peers in the worlds of school and play. This can eventuate in even further withdrawal and alienation.

SUBLIMATION OF DRIVES

Normally, during latency a state of calm pliability and educability ensues, which allows the aggressive and libidinal drives to be sublimated and redirected into productive activities such as learning, playing, and working (Sarnoff, 1976). Although instinctual impulses routinely pressure the ego for expression, creating a wake of increased tension and a generalized state of discomfort, the child learns to transform these demands into socially appropriate channels and, therefore, begins to achieve gratification of the id impulses while simultaneously satisfying the superego.

Hartmann (1954) notes that the sexualization of ego functions interferes with its capacity to perform. The sexually violated child who experiences the direct expression of raw impulses for such behavior is both encouraged and modelled by the parental object. Instead of sublimating sexual drives into typical latency activities involving whole body movements such as swimming, biking, rope jumping, and wrestling, the exploited child is prematurely engaging in actual genital activities. Moreover, rather than neutralizing the drives through competitive activities, or age-appropriate compulsions, reflected by collecting baseball cards, coins, or dolls, the youngster's aggressive impulses break through. The youngster experiences consuming feelings of guilt, helplessness, low self-esteem, poor self-image, self-hate, self-blame, and confusion and often displays these emotions through temper tantrums, fighting, rebellious actions, and self-destructive acts.

UTILIZATION OF PLAY AND FANTASY

Other latency age-appropriate defensive maneuvers that serve as the basis for productive adult functioning may also be thwarted as a result of sexual victimization. Significant to this period is the utilization of fantasy and specific play activities as tools to assist the youngster in mastering the anxieties and demands particular to this stage. Fantasy is one way the youngster discharges drive energies. "It provides . . . the functions that create and support imagination . . . future planning and creative planning" (Sarnoff, 1976, p. 152).

Play, the first step towards sublimation (Peller, 1954), is the essential work of childhood. Youngsters take it seriously and invest a great deal of emotional energy into it. Play assists children in "assimilating piecemeal an experience which was too large to be assimilated instantly in one swoop" (Waelder, 1933, p. 218). Latency-age children tend to use play objects such as board games, action figures, building and drawing materials as mechanisms to learn the skills necessary to master their environment.

The manner in which a child learns to deal with the rules of a game has its parallel in living responsibly. It signifies the child's acceptance of society's norms as well as the child's understanding of his or her rights and privileges in relation to those of others. Games create a safe and permissive climate in which children can experiment with new behaviors. The rules by which sexually abused children learn to live, however, are often confusing, inconsistent, and at odds with peer experiences. As such, the normal satisfactions, gratifications, and opportunities available through play are not accessible to these children. They are inhibited in their capacity to use this modality as a tool that strengthens ego functions, for in the aftermath of trauma, their tendency to use play becomes compulsively repetitive (Terr, 1984). Therefore these children are unable to utilize play either to relieve anxieties or to develop new coping strategies. Instead, the activity takes on a driven quality lacking the usual joy of childhood. We suspect that for some victims, the inception of the developmental progression of anhedonia may even take root at this point.

IDENTIFICATION WITH THE AGGRESSOR

Instead of developing and deploying age-appropriate ego maneuvers, children who have been sexually misused by an important figure in their lives begin to overuse primitive defenses such as identification with the aggressor. This is the ego's strongest defense to counter anxiety generated by an act the child perceives as assaultive (A. Freud, 1966). Through this identification the youngster internalizes a component of the person who initially evoked the anxiety. In so doing, the child assimilates the occurrence, thereby transforming his or her passivity by imitating the aggressor's behavior. The youngster becomes the actor, rather than the victim upon whom the action was foisted.

ALTRUISTIC SURRENDER

In contrast, some sexually misused children never appear to identify with the aggressor as a means of coping with the trauma. They act quite the opposite, overly ingratiating themselves to others—exerting all of their energies in understanding and in pleasing the aggressors. Their own gratifications and satisfactions look as if they are ignored. Winnicott might view this as the basis for the formation of a "false self" in which the child acts is if he or she were selfless. However, we wonder if such behavior might not be what Anna Freud (1966) labels "altruistic surrender," which has an adaptive function. Through this mechanism a youngster fulfills normally unacceptable instinctual aims by projecting these impulses onto another and then, in turn, helping the other person to achieve satisfaction.

The major defense used in "altruistic surrender" is projection, which is generally defined as unacceptable negative impulses thrust on another enabling one to disown the original impulse. Anna Freud (1966) points out that this defense may well serve another function. Namely, it may assist in consolidating interpersonal relationships by helping the abused victim to form positive attachments otherwise unavailable to him or her. This interest in the other is a creative modulation of the impulses and drives, for the id becomes satisfied in spite of superego's objections. The downside to this, though, is that the exploited individual does not initiate self-directed satisfactions. This individual is always helping another and denying the existence of his or her own aspirations.

INHIBITION OF SELF-CARING FUNCTIONS

Development of Self-caring Functions

As children normatively move into latency, they gradually assume more care for their own bodies. They increasingly guard themselves against harm for, by this age, they have introjected many of the parental protective functions.

Because children now have greater interactions outside the home, the parents become less directly involved with them in issues of body safety. In addition, by this stage of development, children's advancing ego functions enable them to become more responsible for themselves. They are now more reality based and have the cognitive apparatus to understand cause and effect (A. Freud, 1966). As such, upon reaching latency, normally developing youngsters are able to make age-appropriate judgments as to the potential risk incurred by their various behaviors. In addition, when faced with somewhat stressful situations, they have the capacity to draw upon a developed repertoire of behaviors to help soothe themselves. They may take a favorite toy from the closet; they may engage in hair twirling or substitute masturbatory activities.

Consequence of Sexual Abuse in Self-care

The ability to exercise the self-caring functions of self-soothing and self-protection assumes that "good-enough" parenting has been internalized. The child has learned to attend to internal cues because attention was given to them in his or her earlier development. Very often, however, the sexually abused youngster is not only exploited by the perpetrator, but also has a disturbed relationship with the nonabusing parent(s). This means that concern for his or her comfort and on-going well-being may have been totally absent or sorely lacking. More often than not, the mother in an incestuous home lacks normal parental empathy and is unattuned to her youngster. The sexually abused child then becomes unable to carry out age-suitable self-caring functions in a self-preserving manner because this function was never provided for him or her.

As a result, we may see a youngster who repeatedly places her or himself in dangerous situations, who self-mutilates and/or engages in other self-destructive activities. This behavior can be interpreted as self-directed rage because the self is experienced as damaged and, therefore, shameful. The unacceptable parts of the self are felt as a perpetual weight that must be removed. The child who engages in "delicate cutting" and other self-harmful behaviors is motivated not by guilt, but rather by feelings of deadness, shame, and profound emptiness (White & Weiner, 1986). When children are sexually misused, they expect to be able to ward off the attacks. When they do not, feelings of self-contempt develop. These emotions are often translated into self-torturing activities, somatization, and/or general overconcern about body integrity and intactness. Sexually exploited children often become overly cathected to their bodies and unduly invested in each ache, pain, or small bruise.

COGNITIVE DYSFUNCTION

Normative Cognitive Functions

The concept of cognition is multifaceted and complex, containing all aspects included in "knowing." It starts with sensory perception and expands to every facet of reasoning. The cognitive process involves intelligence, which Wechsler (as cited in Matarazzo, 1980) conceptualizes as the ability to act with purpose, to use reason, and to interact adequately with one's world. During latency, the cognitive capacities that develop include symbolic functions, secondary process thinking, and concrete operations. In addition, there is the further development of perception, memory, learning, and affects. Moreover, as a result of the consolidation of earlier phases, the latency youngster also becomes increasingly reality-based.

Interference with Clear Thinking

Youngsters who are faced with sexual abuse are forced to confront an event over which they may have no recourse or escape. In this situation, the cognitive apparatus is overwhelmed by fear and anguish. These victims lose the capacity to sift through and extract a solution from their established repertoire of strategies. They become increasingly constricted in their range of responses and therefore become limited in overall functioning. The capacity to self-observe and make appropriate accommodations and corrections, and to anticipate future events and reactions, are lost. Krystal (1988) believes that trauma can be linked to an overall inhibition of mental functioning, thereby leading to a diminished ability to deal effectively with the world.

Piaget (1979) writes that abused children understand their pain and anxiety in accordance with their cognitive development. Youngsters in the midst of latency will therefore interpret sexual abuse in concrete terms. In other words, they will take what is visible at face value and relate it to the reason that they are being victimized. Very often, because they are not yet capable of abstract thinking, children will apply an erroneous explanation to the abuse, somehow blaming themselves for it. In most instances, healthy children pursue pleasure and avoid pain. Since pain becomes tinged with internal meaning, it is often charged with anxiety (A. Freud, 1952). Most youngsters attribute idiosyncratic meaning to a pain-filled event. This can be seen most especially with sexually abused children, who commonly experience physical injury. These youngsters may erroneously link the cause of the pain to some "bad" behavior in which they previously engaged or to some perceived self-flaw.

Distortion of Memory Functions

Memory is another important function that is further developed during latency. During these years, children begin to memorize multiplication tables, the alphabet, the spelling of words, and the rules of mathematics. Traumatized youngsters may compulsively memorize, using this behavior to block out the horror in which they live, and a compulsive personality style may begin to take hold. School may be experienced as the only sanctuary.

When we consider sophisticated aspects of memory that incorporate configurations of events, as opposed to rote memorization, the implications are even more profound. The sexually abused child in having to deal with emotionally charged issues, rather than objective symbols such as numbers, is severely affected. Over time, memories become more and more distorted and repressed. Terr (1989) states that repeated or ongoing traumatic experiences lead to blurred and distorted recollections. As the child grows older, the distorted memories may result in psychological consequences. The distortion may lead to the belief that he or she initiated the sexual encounter. This has the potential to engender tremendous guilt and self-deprecation. In addition, if the memory of the abuse is repressed, while the associated affect remains in consciousness, the child may become estranged from the experiences and from the reasons for his or her feelings.

Estrangement from Feelings

This estrangement has multiple consequences for these child-victims, one of which is an interference in the child's use of symbolic functions. Demers-Desrosiers (1982) notes that the inability to experience one's own emotions eventuates in the virtual incapacity to create mental images, drawings, writings, and music—all expressions that rely upon the use of symbols. When symbols are unavailable cognitively, they become voiced through somatization. In sexually abused children who develop this constellation of symptoms, we see a myriad of physical ailments and complaints. Moreover, sexually assaulted youngsters who repress their emotions in a desperate attempt to survive are, in effect, robbed of the rich expression of their feelings through the metaphor of symbols.

Effect on Secondary Process Thinking

More generally, children may become unable to use secondary process thinking and may regress to primary process, thereby depicting a breech in their capacities to deploy logic and to distinguish both between reality and fantasy and between inner and outer worlds. They may begin to have visual, auditory, or tactile hallucinations, which represent a deterioration in their abilities to use imagery in a growth-enhancing and adaptive manner. Terr (1984) has found that in some cases the traumatized child will incorporate the whole person. When the attacker becomes internalized as a result of a trauma, there is the risk that magical thinking may be triggered, leading the victim to believe he or she is possessed or controlled by a superhuman force.

CASE STUDY ANALYSIS OF DRAWINGS

The remainder of this chapter is devoted to looking at how these break-downs in youngsters' ego strengths are manifested through abused children's projective drawings. In analyzing the House, Tree, Person, and Kinetic Family Drawings created by misused children within six months of their abuse, images of the ego damage they have sustained will be graphically portrayed. While there may be other interesting and noteworthy aspects in each of the renderings, for the purpose of this chapter, we will focus exclusively on those items that reflect disturbances and strengths in ego structure.

Carole

This first drawing, Plate 8, depicts ego dysfunction and was penciled by 6-year-old Carole. She was violated by her father by being forced to view pornographic videos while lying in bed at his side. It is not clear how many times this occurred nor for how long. Soon after the last of these events, her parents separated, and in the process, her mother became extremely depressed and incapable of functioning. Carole tried to care for her mother and assumed full responsibility for her 4-year-old brother, Evan. These circumstances blended together and led to the impairment of her ego.

The most striking feature of Carole's drawing is her treatment of the head, the body part most commonly associated with the ego (Machover, 1980; Ogdon, 1977). Generally speaking, we expect to see exaggerated head sizes in the drawings of 4-year-olds. By the time a youngster reaches Carole's age, she or he is more reality-based. As such, a head as large as the torso is considered unusual (Hammer, 1980). When we couple the enlarged head with the reinforced hairline, we see a picture of a child who is struggling to contain her impulses through ego defenses.

The break between the head and body (the head is not attached to the body) may graphically represent Carole's deployment of the defense mechanism of isolation. Isolation is a means through which an individual copes by separating ideas from the feelings with which they were initially connected. Carole's use of this particular defense alerts us to the possible process of emotional numbing, which is one of the ways that many sex abuse victims cope with feelings and anxiety too overwhelming to otherwise handle. A major consequence of the habitual use of this defense may be the development of alexithymia,

PLATE 8.

which, as we said earlier, is an inability to differentiate affects and/or to become psychologically anesthetized.

Because Carole has struggled to survive by blocking her affects, a state of passivity has ensued wherein she has unconsciously traded a condition of excitation and anxiety for one of surrender. We see this state portrayed in her drawing by the lack of well-defined hands and the presence of mittenlike representations. This hand treatment often connotes the repression of aggressive feelings and actions along with the outward appearance of compliance. Carole has taken on the care of her mother and brother but, in so doing, has forsaken an essential part of herself, including her outrage at both parents. She appears to manifest the characteristics of "altruistic surrender," wherein she is pleasing those immediately around her while denying the satisfaction of her own needs.

David

David is a 5-year-old boy from an upper-middle-class family. He is in the center position of his siblings, having one older and two younger brothers. The sibling born about the time of the onset of David's sexual abuse was diagnosed with Down's Syndrome, a problem which preoccupied the parents, leaving David emotionally ignored. The sexual abuse that progressed from fondling to anal penetration was perpetrated by David's nursery school janitor. It occurred over a period of time. David's disclosure and retelling of the events was consistent with the results of a medical examination.

One of the major tasks in ego development during latency is to sublimate impulses, thereby creating a calm and educative emotional state. When we begin to examine David's rendition of the human figure (Plate 9), our eye is

PLATE 9.

immediately drawn to the striped clothing. The lines on the appendages express his difficulty in controlling his impulses (Ogdon, 1977). As his impulses break through, as depicted by the heavily shaded hair (Urban, 1963), they generate a high level of anxiety for David. He struggles to master this by identifying with the aggressor, another common defense used by abused children. The prisonlike uniform, in which the figure is dressed, reflects this defensive maneuver since David believes that the janitor is in jail.

Another ego function that is adversely affected by sexual abuse is the ability to think clearly. Hanging above the figure's head, the area that houses thoughts, is a metaphoric dark cloud generated by the shadow of David's torment. This shaded cloud represents the youngster's anxiety and depression (Jolles, 1971). The messy hair in this drawing tells us that David's thinking is confused, and the clouds represent the aftermath of the violation, looming above him and preoccupying his thoughts.

Jane

The Person Drawing (Plate 10) by 10-year-old Jane was created as part of her psychological intake at a local clinic. Jane was presenting a cadre of symptoms including nightmares, eating and sleeping disturbances, and ongoing vomiting, all of which appeared to have no medical basis. Jane's parents separated when she was 8 months old, and she remained in the custody of her mother with regular visitation by her father. The youngster seemed problem free until the age of 10, when she disclosed a disturbing visit with her father at his job: He took her to a room with a computer and a couch. While she was playing with the computer, he laid down on the couch. She reports that he unzipped his pants and ordered her to come close to him. He then grabbed her and placed her on top of him, rubbing his penis against the lips of her vagina.

PLATE 10.

Jane's drawing depicts the likely effect of this one incident upon her ego functioning. We see the graphic portrayal of her inner struggle to maintain control over her sexual drives through the wide belt strapped across the body. The belt symbolizes her sexual preoccupation as well as her struggle over her sexual behavior (Ogdon, 1977). On this figure, the belt is pointing towards the genitals giving us yet another clue to this conflictual area. In addition, the total shape of the female torso is clearly phallic, which suggests that Jane's ego is ill prepared to integrate the abusive experience.

As a latency-age youngster, Jane's libidinal drives should be neutralized, allowing for a state of "calm, educability and pliability" (Sarnoff, 1976). However, we see anxiety breaking through her defenses in the treatment of the tightly curled and shaded hair. The erasure at the hand is further evidence of her difficulty in handling the inner tension resulting from the abuse. Jane's figure states "my computer is broken," attesting to the confused thinking which is seen again in the transparent arms. The arms tell us that her way to reaching out into the world is distorted and unrealistic.

Ralph

Plate 11 represents the second phallic body produced by a child asked to draw a picture of a person. This one, drawn by 5-year-old Ralph, is brimming with indications of sexuality gone amuck. Ralph is an identical twin who was physically and sexually abused by his father and his father's girlfriend. The molestation consisted of exposure to pornographic movies, objects forced into his anus, and needles inserted into his toes and penis. The physical violations were confirmed through medical examination. In addition, his father and aunt

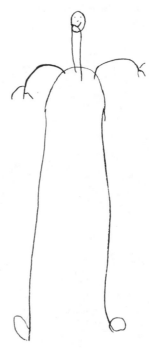

PLATE 11.

took pictures of him naked in his bedroom. Ralph revealed that his father threateningly showed him a brown egg and warned that if he or his brother told anyone what they were doing, he would crack the egg and kill the chick growing within it.

The Person Drawing appears frightening. The arms and hands hover menacingly as if to ward off intruders. Ralph seems to be identifying with the aggressive posture of his father. This is his way of coping and trying to develop the self-caring function of protecting his body from harm. However, it is easy to see that this is a thin veneer presented in order to defend against his intense feelings of helplessness, which are also represented in the drawing. The figure stands quite precariously balanced on feeble sticklike legs. The legs are drawn with a single thin line, with a break in each near the top, which further confirms the powerlessness he experienced (Hammer, 1954) when unable to protect himself against the extreme violation.

A second striking feature is the thin and elongated neck which is associated with feelings of body weakness and organ inferiority "with a compensatory drive or reaction formation towards physical power or aggression tendencies" (Ogdon, 1977, p. 79). This type of neck also connotes Ralph's attempt to separate his thoughts from his emotions, since these feelings contribute to his problems controlling his impulses. The tiny head in relation to the huge phallic body, however, tells us that his impulses are winning the battle for control and overrunning his ability to use his intellect.

Roger

Roger, Ralph's identical twin, was the unfortunate recipient of the same abuse foisted upon his brother. What is particularly noteworthy, however, is the different reactions each child had to the trauma. Both boys were treated at a local child guidance clinic once the abuse was revealed. While Ralph easily recounted the events that took place with his aunt and father, Roger sat silently by his side and shrugged his shoulders sadly when asked if he recalled the same events. Roger neither disputed nor acknowledged his brother's statements. He appeared overcome with shame, inhibiting his capacity to elaborate on his feelings or thoughts. Although these twins look exactly alike, their internal world is markedly divergent. This is revealed by both their behavior and their drawings.

Ralph presents a menacing figure whose impulses have gone wild and whose controls are strained to their limits. Roger, on the other hand, drew two figures (Plate 12 and Plate 13) whose robotlike quality shows successful restraint. Roger struggles to control, or box in, his feelings and impulses. Although he is effective in keeping his impulses at bay, the cost is his disconnection from his feelings—emotional numbness. He is not only alienated from himself but, as important for a latency-age child, keeps himself distant from others. The single, second-floor window in Plate 14 projects his withdrawal from the world (Jolles, 1964). No one is tall enough to look within; he is therefore able to remain aloof.

We note that this same dynamic is present in the Tree Drawing (Plate 15). The crown and branch structure is associated with one's ability to interact and derive satisfaction from the environment (Buck, 1981). "Outer parts of the

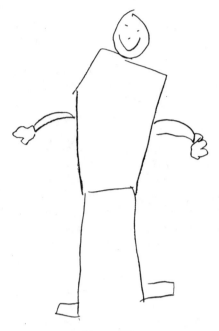

PLATE 12.

PLATE 13.

PLATE 14.

PLATE 15.

crown, the extremities, form the zone of contact with the environment, the zone of relationship and exchange between what is within and what is without" (Koch, 1952, p. 5). Like the window in Plate 14, everything remains out of reach. The enclosed structure of the crown is encapsulating and does not allow the entrance of outside forces. It also prohibits the branch structure from reaching out into the vicinity and reaping any possible benefits.

Remarkable to Roger's drawings is the tenuous connection between the crown and the tree trunk. While it is normal for a 5-year-old to draw a line separating the crown from the trunk (Koch, 1952), the space created by Roger emphasizes a division. It graphically portrays the foliage's disconnection from the nourishing juices of the trunk. The trunk is an accepted representation of the ego (Buck, 1981). The gap between the two tree parts may, therefore, mirror Roger's inability to self-care, an important ego function. This may also explain the description Roger gives in the PDI that the circles or fruits on the crown are oranges. Like the oranges, he has developed a thick skin to protect his fragile interior. Similarly, the boxy torsos (Plates 12 and 13) shield the vulnerable self from the world. These squared-off bodies represent Roger's attempt to hold things in, in order to keep himself together, not fall apart, and not act on his impulses.

Another defense Roger utilizes is denial. Like many other abuse victims, he literally draws a happy picture. Both the Human Figure Drawings (Plates 12 and 13) and the Kinetic Family Drawing (Plate 16) present people wearing a smile.

PLATE 16.

Yet, the other parts of the figures belie these joyful expressions. Particularly, in the KFD, the family members look much like unrooted flowers waiting to be plucked. Roger's distress is further echoed in the HFDs, where we note the short, flimsily connected arms. Machover (1980) states that arms and hands refer to "ego development and social adaptation. It is with arms and hands that we feed, dress, perform skills, explore our body and contact persons about us. It is with arms that we love and caress, hurt and kill, disrupt and adapt" (p. 60). Roger's treatment of arms in his drawings depicts his difficulty in ego development and socialization. However, we also notice that, despite their weakness, the arms extend outward into the environment representing his desire for contact. Sadly, however, his ability to achieve this is impaired. This helplessness is further confirmation of the message conveyed by the encapsulated branch structure in Plate 15.

A final noteworthy point is the reflection of Roger's anxiety. A huge cloud runs the width of the drawing in Plate 14, looming above the house. Beneath it floats a smaller but menacing one. Clouds represent the artist's anxiety (Hammer, 1954). As such we see that despite Roger's efforts to deny and defend against his feelings, anxiety breaks out and shadows his home environment.

Alice

It is unclear what the precise details of 6-year-old Alice's sexual victimization were. We do know that it culminated with her mother coming home from food shopping to find Alice bleeding from the vagina. All Alice was able to reveal was that "my stepfather choked me down there." Medical examination found evidence of vaginal penetration. The legal system ultimately charged and found her mother guilty of neglect. In fact two years earlier Alice had told her mother that her stepfather was molesting her but her mother was unresponsive. Subsequently, Alice and her three younger siblings were placed in four separate foster homes. The drawings discussed here were produced while Alice was living in foster care and attending a local clinic for psychotherapy.

It is significant that Alice drew two human figures without torsos. The sex of each of the figures was identified by Alice (Plate 17, girl; Plate 18, boy).

PLATE 17.

PLATE 18.

According to Koppitz (1968), by the age of 6, 94 percent of girls include the torso in their person drawing. Alice is known to have above average intelligence according to the results of a psychological battery of tests, which included the WISC-R. We can, therefore, surmise that the absent torsos were not the result of cognitive limitations. Alice's omission is clearly related to her sexual victimization and points to her use of denial. She uses this primitive defense mechanism in an attempt to keep unconscious the painful experience to which she was subjected. Levick (1983) notes that the absence of body parts, when the artist is capable of including them, is a graphic manifestation of denial.

Denial is a defense that is typically used by children younger than Alice. Her regression back to this earlier method of protecting her ego from anxiety is further demonstrated in her treatment of the figure's mouth in Plate 17. The emphasis on this body part and its open position indicates a regression and suggests her intense neediness (Urban, 1963). This is additionally substantiated by the Post-Drawing Interview in which she states that the figures need buttons. Buttons connote strong dependency needs for one's mother (Jolles, 1971). This is normal for a 6-year-old, but their exclusion in the drawing, coupled by Alice's comment, leads us to conclude that she experiences conflict about having her needs fulfilled. This is further reflected by the agitated line quality of the mouth (Plate 17).

Both Person Drawings seem to indicate that Alice feels she cannot count on others to care for her. Sadly, she draws herself without a body, arms, legs, or feet, leaving only a head, neck, and shoulders with which to care for herself. Her intellect, as represented by the large head, has served her well, but without the other parts she is left severely handicapped to negotiate life's demands.

Nancy

Eight-year-old Nancy began treatment at a local child guidance clinic after sustaining four years of sexual abuse by her stepfather. The violation was uncovered after she complained about a brown discharge and burning from her vagina. She was taken, by her grandmother, to a hospital emergency room where she was diagnosed with vaginal, anal, and oral gonorrhea. She told authorities that her stepfather touched her in her private parts with his penis. She also revealed that she had told her mother about the sexual activity when it began but, at that time, her mother called her a liar. Presently, Nancy is living with her maternal aunt and uncle. Her mother still is hard-pressed to believe that Nancy was raped by her own husband. Tragically, Nancy longs to be reunited with her mother and indicated her wish to "see my mother every day, every weekend and to go back home" in the PDI.

Nancy presents us with a female figure (Plate 19) who appears to be wearing a mask. As we said earlier, a common sequelae for the victim of sexual abuse is

PLATE 19.

the development of alexithymia or emotional numbing. Feelings that are too overpowering to be handled are blocked and a veneer of complacency is put on. The abused child masks feelings both to herself and others. It may be that a false complying self is presented to the world while unconsciously a sense of powerlessness and anger loom. Nancy demonstrates this quite poignantly in her Person Drawing. The face looks like a flattened mask pretending joy (note smile). Since the only erasure on the page is on the face, her worry over the mask's perfect presentation is suggested. We note, however, that the figure wears her heart, precariously hanging from a single string, over her constricted chest. Numb to her true feelings, her heart, nonetheless, stands exposed and vulnerable.

Nancy attempts to compensate for this vulnerability, against which she feels helpless to mitigate, by acting strong. We see this echoed in her rendering of the figure's shoulders (Plate 19), which look oversized and padded, resonating her overconcern about her need for strength and power (Jolles, 1971). This contrasts with the male figure she drew (Plate 20), which is about half the size of the female figure. The male figure has a frail, thin body and, despite broad shoulders, connotes helplessness through his short, stubby arms. This male also wears glasses, indicating that he needs help to see. Even with this assistance, though, he still has only one pupil and is therefore blind in one eye. This man may portray Nancy's utilization of reaction formation, an age-appropriate defense, which represents a degree of health on her part. This mechanism is a process by which an unacceptable feeling or idea is repressed and replaced with its exaggerated opposite in consciousness. Nancy's drawing of a relatively weak man serves to protect her from experiencing both her underlying anxiety regarding the abuse and her own painful feelings of shame.

PLATE 20.

Jack

Six-year-old Jack was sexually abused from age 3 to 5 by his father, who was then the principal of a local public school. Although the full extent of the type of exploitation is not clear, there was medical evidence indicating that the youngster had been violated by anal penetration. This sexual infraction was uncovered by his mother after she inadvertently found Jack engaging in oral sex and attempting genital sex with his 7-year-old sister. At the time of the projective drawing test, the parents had separated and both children were living with their mother. Their father, who had relocated to another state, was in the process of suing for custody, denying any charges of sexual molestation.

We see in Jack's House Drawing (Plate 21) a triangular-shaped building. More commonly drawn by 4-year-olds (Kellogg, 1969), the constricted structure possibly represents a lag in Jack's cognitive development. Since there is no evidence of any neurological impairment, we can conclude that this cognitive deficit is emotionally based. This type of house symbolizes Jack's inability to interact adequately with his world. Just as the house narrows and thereby has limited space towards the roof, the range of Jack's behaviors and responses have become restricted as a result of the abuse.

We see a phallic protrusion emanating from the lower right portion of the house. This clearly delineated shape may well suggest that Jack is isolating his feelings about the sexual abuse and splitting them off from his thoughts in an effort to ward off guilt, shame, and anxiety about his actions. In a sense, he is relegating these emotions to a small, definitive corner, keeping them separated from the rest of his world. However, their existence was corroborated in the Post-Drawing Interview in answer to the question, "What is the worst part of the house?" Jack answered, "The back door, cause it's all dirty inside and needs to be cleaned up." This may reflect the way Jack experiences his own body, particularly his anus which was sexually penetrated. He feels filthy and shameful.

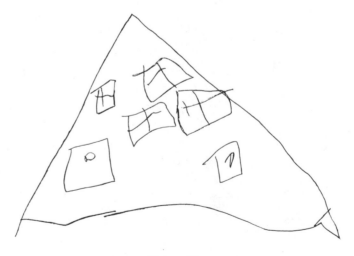

PLATE 21.

Jessica

Ten-year-old Jessica was victimized by her grandfather. He confessed to exposing himself, fondling her genitals, and masturbating while she observed him. This same man sexually abused his daughter, Jessica's mother, when she was a child. Jessica's older brother was also a victim of the grandfather. He sustained greater abuses than Jessica, including exposure, fondling, masturbation, and digital and penile anal penetration. The extended maternal family (including the grandfather) lived upstairs from Jessica in a shared two-family house, thereby leaving the children readily accessible to the grandfather's violations which extended over several years.

The house drawn by Jessica (Plate 22) presents a confused picture. The main part of the building faces frontward, giving the observer a one-dimensional view. Jessica's house has a simple façade, including most essential details. Solid walls, windows with panes, and a door complete with doorknob are all present, demonstrating inner resources which enable Jessica to produce what is expected. However, the treatment of the roof belies this uncomplicated image. The wavy line separating the roof from the rest of the house suggests a shaky boundary between the way in which she appears to the world and her inner thoughts. Here, in the roof, in the area that symbolizes fantasies and may reflect "conditions in which fantasy distorts one's mental functioning" (Hammer, 1980, p. 173), she creates a triple perspective that violates the logical thinking developmentally appropriate for her age. It is no accident that the breakdown in logical thinking appears in the roof, for this youngster is struggling to integrate the reality of the sexual abuse within the construct of her self.

PLATE 22.

Jessica's PDI story states that "the house has a new porch and there's a hole underneath to hide." This may represent her current attempt to repress or hide from the trauma she experienced. Yet, her anxiety peeks through the façade of the house's main structure via the shaded doorknob. The special attention to this area, seen nowhere else in the drawing, illustrates her phallic preoccupation (Buck, 1981) and a possible breakthrough of her libidinal drives.

Another defense Jessica calls upon to combat against her inner conflict is displacement. This is reflected in the PDI by Jessica's identification of the house as belonging to her brother's friend. By this ego maneuver Jessica is distancing herself in an attempt to master her overwhelming affects and anxieties.

Elmer

Seven-year-old Elmer was sexually fondled and intimately kissed by his paternal uncle three months before the projective drawing tests were administered. Sadly, this is repetitive of his father's childhood in which he, too, was sexually abused during latency. Fortunately, Elmer and his mother enjoy a relatively positive relationship, which enabled the youth to tell her about the molestation. His mother took immediate action, securing both psychological and medical help for Elmer. She also stopped any contact between him and his uncle.

When we look at Elmer's drawings of a tree (Plate 23) and human figure (Plate 24), we are struck by the excessive detailing in each. This unusual

PLATE 23.

presentation connotes the youngster's need to somehow structure the dangerous environment in order to ward off his anxiety (Hammer, 1980). In the
Post-Drawing Interview, Elmer refers to the poison flowers flanking the tree as
well as the poisonous berries growing on it. No wonder he feels the need to
protect himself. Already experiencing himself as venomous, as seen through
his projective use of "poison berries," he gives further testimony to his internal
marring by creating a tree whose trunk appears to be cut off. Since the trunk is
a reflection of one's ego strength (Ogdon, 1977), Elmer's truncated trunk implies
that his developing ego functions have been abruptly curtailed, resulting in
inadequate defenses.

Elmer's inability to adequately defend against the flooding of his inner
tensions is projected by the number of clouds present in both renderings
(Jolles, 1971), the heavily shaded body on the Person Drawing, and the shaded
owl in the tree's hole. The very existence of this hole, or scar, indicates an
earlier trauma, suggesting a possible reason for Elmer's agitation. Last, we
cannot help but notice the thin and transparent roots which look pitifully
incapable of stabilizing a tree of that size. They connote how tenuously Elmer
is maintaining his grasp of reality and just how flimsy his hold on it may be.

Lois

Lois is another child who lives in a household with extended family members. This 7-year-old resides with her parents, a 3-year-old sister, and her maternal grandmother and uncle. The family occupies a two-family home, with the nuclear family in one apartment and her mother's family in the other. Lois disclosed that her 14-year-old male cousin had exposed himself to her, observed her naked, fondled her, and then masturbated in front of her. This series of abusive interactions lasted for over one year. The cousin subsequently confessed, at which time the maternal grandmother also admitted that she had been molested by her uncle when she was a child.

Lois's Tree Drawing (Plate 25) gives clear indication that she is a child who has fallen victim to trauma. In this drawing, we notice that the trunk is two-dimensional, while the branches are drawn with single, one-dimensional lines. This connotes good early development that is interrupted by a later trauma (Jolles, 1971). The presence of trauma is also manifested by the

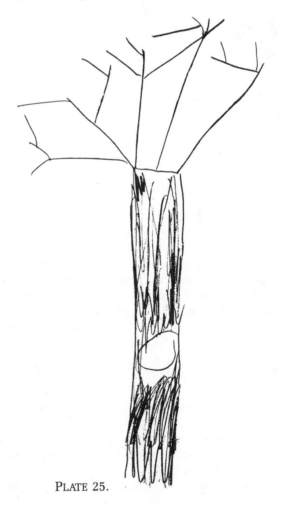

PLATE 25.

existence of the tree's scar or hole. Additionally, in her female Person Drawing (Plate 26) we observe a strange thinning of the hair at the crown. This phenomenon is one which has not been documented elsewhere, but it is one that the authors have seen as a detail frequently present in the Person Drawings of sexually abused youngsters. As such, we believe it may be a significant indice of sexual trauma.

The effects of the traumatic experience upon Lois's ego are not only in her two Person Drawings, but also in her Tree Drawing. Since the tree trunk is an index of basic ego strength (Buck, 1981), the lightly sketched sides portend a feeling of impending ego breakdown. This fear of the shattering and collapse of her ego is not unfounded. The placement of the scar threatens the integrity of the trunk, thereby symbolizing how the trauma has overwhelmed her ego. Another aftermath of the trauma is the flooding of Lois's ego with anxiety. This pressure is reflected by the dark shading (Di Leo, 1970) especially present in her female Person and Tree Drawings. Although both figures wear a smiling face depicting the denial of her devastating feelings, the shaded details reveal that Lois's inner tensions cannot be contained.

Lois's use of denial is also depicted in the way she represents the torso. It has been noted that the absence of a trunk suggests both anxiety and denial of body drives (Jolles, 1971; Koppitz, 1968). In both Person Drawings, the trunk is suggested, but only minimally through single lines. The immature presentation is very clear in the male Person Drawing (Plate 27) and, upon close scrutiny, is

PLATE 26.

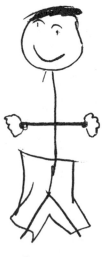

PLATE 27.

also apparent in the female Person Drawing (Plate 26), where it has been covered over by a heavily shaded shirt. Although the body is therefore represented, it is drawn in a constricted way, implying that while Lois is attempting to deny her bodily impulses, the maneuver is not effective. Her impulses break through as evidenced by the heavily shaded hair, the jagged bangs, and the shirtless male figure (Plate 27). Her struggle to maintain control is also represented by the extremely elongated necks on both figures. It is as if Lois's ego were stretched to its limit in an attempt to separate the pressure of her drives from her thoughts.

The full extent of this untenable position has forced Lois to deny reality and instead to utilize a regressed mode of thinking. The transparencies indicate that she periodically reverts to primary process thinking. Her judgment becomes impaired and her perceptions become distorted.

Dennis

Six-year-old Dennis was not abused by a family member, but rather by an 18-year-old male neighbor who ultimately confessed to the molestation. At the time of the abuse, Dennis's family was plagued with financial difficulties, which had begun when a fire destroyed the family home. This crisis was followed by other financial misfortunes which caused the father to increase his working hours. His absence from the home left Dennis more needy and vulnerable. The child longed for male company, a situation that his neighbor took advantage of. For a period of three months, Dennis was asked to disrobe, to view the perpetrator's naked body, and to engage in mutual fondling. These series of events left their mark on Dennis as we see in his House and Tree Drawings (Plates 28 & 29 respectively).

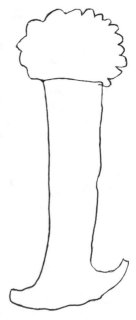

PLATE 28.   PLATE 29.

When we look at the House Drawing (Plate 28), we are struck by the pervasive sense of emptiness. There is no suggestion of life, and a sense of deadness and numbness permeates the environment. Even the chimney, a symbolic representation of family warmth (Buck, 1948) and an item typically present by age 6, is omitted. This emotional numbing is unfortunately one of the legacies of sexual abuse and is typically one of the ways a victim will try to cope with the overwhelming affects that are elicited by the abuse.

Often accompanying this "soul murder," in which a child's inner sense of aliveness is sacrificed, is the outward appearance of an obliging and compliant youngster. Both of Dennis's drawings allude to this defensive posture. With the exception of the chimney, the house as drawn is what would be expected in a rendering by a 6-year-old. The essential details—the walls, door, window, and roof—are all present. It is only under closer observation that problems become apparent. The compliant manner in which Dennis interacts with his environment is also revealed in the rendering of the "arcadelike formation" of the tree's crown (Plate 29). Koch (1952) indicates that this depiction is the way "obliging" individuals tend to draw the branch system.

The root structure in Dennis's tree is most unusual—so much so that none of the literature the authors reviewed referred to this particular type of treatment. However, we have noticed that the rockerlike base is, in fact, periodically present in the tree drawings of sexually traumatized children. We believe that this characteristic, like the thinning of the hair at the crown, may be another marker of sexual abuse.

In trying to understand what this phenomenon symbolizes, we refer to Koch's conclusion (1952) that roots are the metaphoric index of personality stability. In looking at Dennis's tree, one has the sense that it has been taken up from the soil, thereby exposing its circular roots. It has been uprooted from the source of nourishment, groundedness, and security. Although it is drawn standing, the tree's base is shaky and there is the threat that, with the slightest amount of pressure, it could roll sideways. This strongly echoes the devastating effects that trauma has on its victim. It has the potential to decimate ego functions, to knock them down. Dennis's drawing also depicts his resilience, however. Although the tree may falter from its upright position and lean perilously towards the ground, it will right itself eventually because of the rocker base. However, it will also continue to rock and never be quite stable.

Moreover, to continue to stand up after being knocked down is not without profound emotional cost. The stretching of the child's resources to integrate his understanding of the assault into his previous perception of himself and his world has the potential to shatter his sense of efficacy and replace it with feelings of powerlessness, helplessness, and inferiority. The rocking, unstable quality that Dennis has drawn for the base leaves the tree vulnerable to outside forces, Because it is not rooted in the ground, it cannot stand up against hostile elements. It can only bounce back and await the next onslaught, just as the abused victim waits time and again for subsequent assaults.

James

Like many victims of sexual abuse, 10-year-old James has suffered multiple traumas. Beginning at the age of 2, his parents were divorced and the mother, who was young, stressed, and overwhelmed, became physically violent towards him, echoing the manner in which she was treated as a child. She punched James, kicked him, and threw him against the wall repeatedly. His life was trouble-filled from birth since the marriage had been dysfunctional and problematic from the start. His father rejected James and, although he lived close by, rarely saw James after the divorce.

James's mother Joan worked as a barmaid and, after the separation from her husband, she asked the neighbors to watch her son. The neighbors had a history of alcohol abuse and, unbeknownst to Joan at the time, they had been repeatedly reported to the local authorities for allegations of child sexual abuse. While watching James, the 12-year-old daughter from this family forcibly undressed him and then disrobed herself and fondled the youngster. After several months of this activity, he finally told his mother, Joan. Since she was in therapy at the time, she reported it to her therapist, who in turn called child protective services. Joan understood the necessity to shield her son from further assault since she, herself, had been sexually abused by her brothers and their friends through the course of her childhood. As an adult, Joan was actively struggling to master the aftermath of this trauma and its concomitant effects on her mothering ability. Her therapy had helped her reach the point at which she was able to hear James's cry and take appropriate action.

James's drawings of a female (Plate 30) and of his family doing something together (Plate 31) clearly reflect the toll that life experiences have taken on him. His view of women is darkened by anxiety, most particularly in the area of sexuality. This is shown by the heavily shaded bathing suit covering the genitalia of the female figure. Ogdon (1977) states that when a male draws a female that includes an emphasis on the hair, breasts, and bare legs, strong sexual impulses are conveyed. James's drawing of a woman has large breasts, exposed legs, and tightly curled hair. In addition, the open torsos found in James's depiction of himself (middle figure) and his mother (figure on right) in the KFD (Plate 31) are another indication of the pressure of his age-inappropriate sexual concerns (Urban, 1963).

PLATE 30.

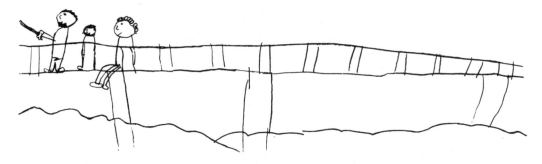

PLATE 31.

James's focus on sexuality seems to be a result of his molestation and of his earlier disturbed relationship with his mother. It may even be that he has eroticized the beatings inflicted on him by his mother, as well as their relationship in general. We notice that the KFD depicts his mother without any sexual characteristics as compared to the bearded father (figure on left), who holds a phalliclike fishing pole. It is possible that James's sexualization of his relationship with his mother is so anxiety-provoking that when he is asked to draw her, he denies her sexuality in total. Again, this is in marked contrast to the sexualization portrayed in the female figure of Plate 30.

A child's representation of the human body has special importance in interpreting the youngster's sense of his or her power in the world (Halpern in Hammer, 1980). In the KFD, as noted above, both James and his mother are depicted with trunks that are open. In James's rendition of himself there is a sense that the body is empty and all that exists, in fact, is the outer shell. It is as if his "self" has been emptied leaving him open and vulnerable. When we turn to his mother, we see a similar representation. The lower part of her body is defined by the pier on which she sits, connoting the perception that she is her environment and is void of a sense of self-definition. We can therefore conclude that not only does James experience himself as powerless, but also he senses that his mother is unable to provide the backup ego strength to compensate for his own deficiencies.

Judith

Seven-year-old Judith, from an upper-middle-class suburban family, is another child sexually abused by a trusted male neighbor. A product of her mother's second marriage, Judith has a much older half brother and sister who no longer lived at home at the time of her abuse. The violations began when she was 4 and continued unabated until her seventh birthday, when the abuse was discovered. It was subsequently confirmed by her pediatrician. Judith was forced into a full gamut of sexual activities, ranging from fondling to fellatio and cunnilingus, to vaginal-penile penetration. Unfortunately, Judith's mother has a diagnosed thought disorder and was thus unable to provide her daughter with the kind of relationship that would have fostered an earlier disclosure. As such, the abuse continued for years.

PLATE 32.

Judith's drawings reflect her desperate attempt to maintain a sense of control over her inner chaos and disorganized world. In her drawing of a tree (Plate 32), the sheer number of birds and apples overwhelms the environment, giving us a gauge of how completely her thoughts and feelings clutter her head. The birds hover around the tree, leaving little room for anything else. The overly abundant apples, outlining the tree's crown and filling its center, portray how her dependency needs consume her. Judith's excessive use of detail connotes her perception of a dangerous world and reflects her battle to maintain ego control (Hammer, 1980). This struggle is also seen through the rigid, rulerlike line of the trunk. There is a sense that Judith is trying to structure her world and thereby control it. In the midst of this confusion, we note that she has placed two flowers flanking each side of the tree in an almost heroic attempt to bring life and balance to her existence. Sadly, they are without leaves for support and protection and stand their ground very tenuously.

Judith's need to order her inner world is also represented in her KFD (Plate 33), in which she depicts her family "outside playing together." Looking at

PLATE 33.

Judith's portrayal of herself, you will notice a dark line around her face. Jolles (1971) states that this is equated with a strong effort to maintain control over upsetting thoughts. Judith's attempts are not all together successful, as her anxiety surfaces in both drawings. We are alerted to this by the excessive details in the Tree Drawing and heavily shaded hair in the KFD. More alarmingly, we note several transparencies in both renderings that are indicative of her breakdown in reality testing and thinking.

Another troublesome flag is Judith's depiction of herself in the KFD. Her body has literally come apart. The chest area, the seat of her feelings, is no longer connected to her genitalia and her sexual drives. The conflict between the expression and control of her drives is so intense that it has broken her apart. She has, in fact, become disconnected from a part of herself. Again, she defensively tries to contain her impulses as seen in the legs of her figure. They are rigidly pressed together, holding back her sexual energies (Jolles, 1964) and keeping out external intrusions. Let us not forget to notice all the smiling faces, which carefully camouflage her trauma.

Tara

Tara is an attractive seven-year-old youngster who, on the day of the drawings, was neatly dressed in pants and a tee shirt. She separated easily from her mother, her mother's boyfriend, and her brother to join the tester in another room. She related to the tester eagerly and was readily engaged in all the tasks. Tara was brought to the clinic after her mother told her pediatrician that she had been sexually abused by her father for the last two years. Tara had revealed to her mother that she and her father were involved in a full range of sexual activities, which included oral, anal, and vaginal sex. He had even purchased sexy undergarments and nightgowns for her to wear with him. Medical evidence confirmed that the child had had anal and vaginal intercourse. This molestation appears to have started after the parents divorced and the father moved to another state. At the time of the interview, the father was suing the mother for custody and the mother was countersuing on the charge of sexual abuse. Unfortunately, the courts were having a hard time believing Tara's story since her father was a reputable member of the community and a respected schoolteacher.

When we look at Tara's three drawings of a house (Plate 34), a person (Plate 35) and a tree (Plate 36), various indicators suggest that this youngster had not successfully entered latency and was pathological in her ego development. During latency, the use of fantasy is integral to the child's ability to repress drives, form identifications, and channel the impulses into productive activities. Tara's drawings attest that she is unable to utilize fantasy appropriately. The house has an empty space where the roof should go, symbolizing her incapacity to fantasize productively and her tendency to confuse fantasy with reality. In her Person Drawing, the hair thinning at the crown is the only shaded area in the person (one of the author's suggested indices of sexual abuse). This again suggests Tara's difficulty in the domain of her thoughts, particularly those involving fantasy.

PLATE 34.

PLATE 35.

PLATE 36.

Tara's inability to keep perspective between what is real and what is in her head is mirrored by the double-perspective house, the transparent root structure of her tree, and the animal floating on the tree trunk. At age 7, she should be able to represent these items more realistically. The fact that she does not connotes that her thinking has become muddled. She presents the observer with all the thoughts that inundate her, filling her drawings with a multitude of details, thus flooding the viewer as well.

We also note the tree on the left of the House Drawing (Plate 34). Its branches are sawed off, representing Tara's inhibition or ineptitude at self-expression (Hammer, 1980). It is as if her own ideas are cut off from herself, yet, at the same time, she has the sense that something is missing (Koch, 1952). Like the tree that once had complete branches, Tara was once in touch with her own thoughts and affects, most likely prior to the abuses by her father and the parental divorce. This is tragically reflected in the PDI to the Tree Drawing, in which Tara describes the branches as dead. This branch treatment not only suggests her experience of trauma, but also projects the loss of her capacity to receive satisfaction from interpersonal relationships. It is probable that this affects and reflects her ability to interact with her peers and use them as both helpmates and playmates. This is another flag that Tara is having difficulty entering latency and developing the ego functions necessary to support this period.

Fantasy partially serves the purpose of mitigating against overwhelming experiences and the concomitant anxiety. In a sense, it provides the latency child with the opportunity to practice, or rework, a situation and diffuse anxiety. However, Tara's use of fantasy through the rendering of clouds and birds suggests that it is not serving this purpose for her. Rather, it reflects her overbearing uneasiness that literally clouds all the environments in which she projects herself. Moreover, the very grounds on which the person and the tree stand are thick with agitation (Plates 35 and 36), suggesting her concern about stability and groundedness. The intensively scribbled crown on the tree in Plate 36 gives further evidence of this inner state (Koch, 1952). Her obsessional style depicted by the detailing is faulty, ineffectively fending off the waves of anxiety that permeate all atmospheres.

Harry

Harry had a rough start from the very beginning. He was born to immature parents caught in the turmoil of a troubled marriage. His father was incapable of controlling his temper. Before his first birthday, Harry had already been physically abused and tortured by this man with beatings and the withholding of feedings. Harry would scream until he threw up. He was also tied to his crib, and when he was 8 months old, his father set fire to the crib. When he was a year old, his mother divorced his father in an attempt to rescue the child from further torment. The next few years were fairly uneventful, with the exception of his mother's remarriage.

At age 5, two separate instances of sexual abuse occurred. In one situation a female baby-sitter slept naked next to him. During this same period, his maternal aunt exposed herself to him and posed provocatively. Both women confessed when confronted. These events triggered Post-traumatic Stress

Disorder in Harry and were manifested through severe nightmares, extreme
clinging to his mother, bouts of intense crying, self-verbalizations that he was
a bad person, and extreme feelings of guilt. Harry's mother, Mary, was alert to
his symptoms since she was also sexually abused as a child by her own mother.
Fortunately, Mary's second marriage to a physician was solid and successful.
His stepfather helped Harry by directing the youngster into therapy. Harry,
now age 10, is a strong student, has received numerous athletic awards, is
popular among his friends, and, from all accounts, has made a successful
adjustment into latency.

   The drawings shown here—Tree (Plate 37), Person (Plate 38), Kinetic Family
Drawing (Plate 39), and House (Plate 40)—were sketched when Harry was 5
years old and had disclosed the abuse only two months earlier. These three
renderings suggest Harry's above-average I.Q. The two-dimensional characteristics of the figure, including arms, legs, feet, the inclusion of a neck, three
items of clothing (shirt, hat, shoes with laces), shown in Plate 38 all imply his
intellectual strength. These items according to Koppitz (1968) are not expected
or common inclusions in the Human Figure Drawings of 5-year-old boys. Their
presence connotes a well-developed cognitive ability. However, while these
drawings are above average quantitatively, qualitatively they reveal the pathology that resulted from Harry's multiple traumas.

   Although Harry appears to possess good intellectual capacities, the drawings suggest that he is unable to utilize these capacities to master his environment and the challenges put forth to him. The size of the hands and arms,
particularly in Plate 38, implies his desire to control and handle his surroundings (Levy, 1950). By the same token, their size also creates an awkwardness

PLATE 37.   PLATE 38.

PLATE 39.

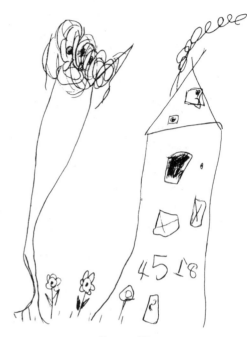

PLATE 40.

that renders them relatively useless. The same dynamic is reflected in the manner in which the tree crown is drawn (Plates 37 and 40). The branch structure is jumbled and confused, suggesting Harry's difficulty in reaching out and directing his interactions with his world. The attention to the roof of the house (Plate 40) demonstrates his proclivity to turn inward rather than seeking fulfillment from the environment. This use of fantasy is positive when it is also balanced with seeking others out for social interactions and satisfactions. Unfortunately, Harry has not achieved this balance and instead overutilizes fantasy.

Related to this interpersonal style is the faint line quality seen in all of Harry's drawings (some drawings were darkened for reproduction). This linear presentation is indicative of the youngster's low energy level and the subsequent tentative manner in which he approaches tasks (Hammer, 1980). In addition, because it also reflects his insecurity and inhibitions, it attests to his inability to initiate activities (Alschuler & Hattwick, 1947). This problem is of particular concern when evident in a latency-age child since, as we discussed earlier, this is one of the major tasks necessary to successfully negotiate this stage of development (Erikson, 1963).

A second major difficulty revealed in Harry's drawings is his problem in controlling his impulses. This impulsivity is exhibited in the tumultuously scribbled tree crowns (Plates 37 and 40), the scribbled beard and horizontal shirt lines in Plate 38, as well as the huge hands on virtually every figure (Plates 38 and 39). The faint lines on the tree trunks mirror his ego's inability to contain these strong impulses (Jolles, 1971). There is some evidence to suggest that the drives pressuring Harry are sexual in nature. This is seen in the agitated beard in the HFD (Plate 38) (Urban, 1963) and in the hair thinning at the crown on this figure as well as on the figures in the KFD (Figure 39).

There is also an indication that Harry is trying to put a cap and a limit on both his fantasies and impulses as seen in the presence of the hat and shoe laces in Plate 38. In fact, the phalliclike flower protruding from horizontal lines on the hat and the shoe laces that offer little support further substantiate his trouble in this area. Of additional note is the particular attention drawn to the shoes by the laces. Shoes are symbolic of the phallus and sexuality. Machover (1980) states that when a shoe has elaborations, such as the laces in this drawing, an emphasis on sexual impulses is present. This certainly would be expected as one of the sequelae of the child who has been sexually abused.

It is heartwarming evidence of the resiliency of children to note that Harry was able to recover from the inner scars of his multiple trauma. Endowed with cognitive strengths, he was able to use them to his advantage and excel in school. In addition, he understood and was able to put in perspective the events of his earlier life. Undoubtedly, this process was fostered by the combination of a good mother-son relationship, a supportive stepfather, and long-term therapeutic intervention. These resources enabled him to eventually function on a level appropriate for his age.

Nadine

Nine-year-old Nadine is another victim of child sexual abuse. Although we have no information beyond the fact that this abuse was validated, her drawings nevertheless provide us with the opportunity to hone in on the difficulties she has encountered in ego development.

An important ego function developed during latency is that of being able to self-direct and become increasingly more independent. We see evidence in Nadine's drawings (Plates 41 to 45) that this was an area with which she struggled but did not master. The figures' arms, in Plates 41 and 42 and on some of the figures in Plate 43, are long. This limb treatment is associated with aggressively seeking out the environment (Koppitz, 1968), externally directed tendencies (Hammer, 1980), and a general tendency towards reaching out to others. While looking towards others for need gratification is perfectly healthy and normal, the elongated arms represent Nadine's intense and unsatisfied craving for others.

This same problem is reflected in the Tree Drawing (Plate 44), in which Nadine draws the crown falling down onto and over the trunk like a sack. Koch (1952) links this style of depicting the tree's crown with individuals who produce nothing from within and instead allow themselves to be driven by others. A third representation of Nadine's lack of self-directedness is projected in her drawing of a vacant house (Plate 45). This house, as an inner self-portrait (Buck, 1981), appears to be devoid of life, empty of self; it is as if no one is home. Nadine is not connected to her own self, including her thoughts, feelings, desires, and wishes.

Last, in Nadine's KFD (Plate 43), she presents us with the five members of her family sitting passively on a couch, doing nothing, very much like the popular couch potato image. It appears that Nadine experiences her entire

PLATE 41.

PLATE 42.

PLATE 43.

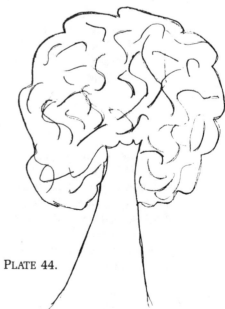

PLATE 44.

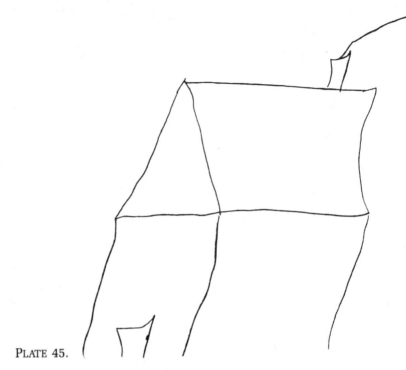

PLATE 45.

family as dependent, infantile, and helpless. They almost become part of the sofa, fading into the environment, barely noticed or noticeable. They lack their own definition and instead become defined by their surroundings.

Another ego dysfunction represented in Nadine's drawings is related to her control of her drives. Although this youngster is disconnected from her feelings, thoughts, and desires, she is nevertheless influenced by them, and there is ample evidence that Nadine is trying to repress them. Hints of her aggressive impulses leak out through the mittenlike hands (Machover, 1980) in Plates 41 and 42. Likewise, the shaded hair on the figures in Plates 41, 42, and 43 project anxiety over her sexuality and fantasy life. A plethora of confused lines fills the crown of the tree (Plate 44), depicting Nadine's inhibited style and lack of clear thinking (Koch 1952). This is particularly distressful when observed in a latency-age child, because understanding cause and effect relationships is a cognitive milestone of this stage. Nadine's inability to do so, coupled with her lack of initiative and difficulty in controlling her drives are evidence that this 9-year-old child has had a difficult time making her entrance into latency. This places her future development at risk and alerts us to her vulnerability in being able to negotiate future life stages.

CONCLUSION

It cannot be overstated that latency is a pivotal time in the child's evolutionary development towards adulthood. The many ego functions that develop and evolve in these critical years serve as the basic structure through which new experiences are understood and incorporated. These become the adult's way of being in the world. However, the sexually molested child not only experiences immeasurable suffering during this crucial period, but also, as the drawings in this chapter have portrayed, the youngster develops dysfunctional ego structures that have the potential to cripple him or her.

CHAPTER 4

ABERRATIONS IN THE SUPEREGO OF SEXUALLY MOLESTED YOUNGSTERS

The superego is that part of the intrapsychic structure that contains the ethical principles and conscience of the individual. Intrinsic to the superego's function is its role in warding off the id's sexual and aggressive impulses by identifying and alerting the ego to potential dangers resulting from a difference between an id demand and moral principle. In the instance of sexual exploitation, the child's impulses are aroused while his or her superego attempts to exert control. The sexual stimulation intensifies existing libidinal pressure and creates internal conflict within the youngster. The child may be aware that the sexual acting out is wrong but feels compelled to comply. The child and the environment are at cross purposes, and he or she, therefore, experiences additional conflict.

GUILT

One of the enduring effects of latency is its modifications of the superego. While the beginnings of the superego construct may occur as early as 6 to 12 months, it is during latency that important transformations take place. These changes endure throughout the life cycle with only modest modifications. Latency is the time when the "motivating affect which characterizes the . . . superego is guilt" (Sarnoff, p. 135). Kessler (1966) defines this feeling as a hurtful emotion that is comprised of both anxiety and aggression. The guilt is pervasive for the child-victim of sexual abuse who feels both culpable and helpless simultaneously.

THE PROCESS OF IDENTIFICATION

All parents have expectations for their youngsters that are conveyed both verbally and nonverbally. However, the parental abuser communicates a bastardization of conventional mores. Over time, assaulted children, as well as youngsters who grow up without abuse, incorporate their parents' values by a complicated process of identification. This ultimately enables children to have a set of internalized standards that replaces those that were formerly external. It is no longer outside punishment that the latency youngster fears but rather the wrath of his or her own superego. Now the punisher has become the self. This process of identification and superego formation becomes pathogenic for the child-victim of sexual abuse who receives contradictory messages about behavioral standards and proper morals.

Parental attitudes and ethics that youngsters initially swallow whole are reassessed during normative latency development by children who are developmentally capable of deciding which parental values to retain and which to discard. Sexually assaulted youngsters have less flexibility in this regard, since a cloud of threats, confused values, torn loyalties, and unresolved oedipal issues hover over them, inhibiting their ability to think rationally or make sound decisions.

During latency, peer influence over youngsters' moral choices and behavior begins to take preeminence. Agemates' attitudes mold a new expanded version of ethical conduct. Children are no longer propelled solely by the earlier goal of pleasing their parents. They are aware of a diversity of views and make choices based on what they feel is right, or on the basis of potential guilt if they elect not to follow parental dictums. Nevertheless, identification with the parent leaves an indelible imprint, despite the influence of these other variables. This is especially significant when we try to understand the aberrant functioning of the superego in sexually traumatized children.

IDENTIFICATION WITH DELINQUENT VALUES

As with the other structures we discussed earlier, superego dysfunctions are dependent upon a constellation of environmental and constitutional factors. These dysfunctions can be characterized under five areas; Redl & Wineman (1957) cite four of these; the first category is the identification of a child with the delinquent values of peers or parents. Children who thus align themselves may appear as if they have no values but, in fact, have introjected distorted codes of behavior. They are actually conforming to their environment and do not see themselves as either bad or rebellious. This type of superego disturbance may be one way in which sexually abused youngsters come to terms with abuse. Behaviorally, they may become sexually provocative to peers, seductive to adults, or bullying to others as they identify with the aggressor. The youngster's ego ideal may potentially be that of a child molester. In this case, the child's self-esteem becomes regulated by his or her ability to sexually satisfy the perpetrator. Sexuality in the adult form, although developmentally premature for this latency child, becomes an embraced value.

Such child-victims are often preoccupied with sexual thoughts and involve themselves with repetitive sexually related acts such as masturbation and sex play. These youngsters instigate sexual contact with peers digitally, orally, and/or genitally. In fact, Bunk and Wabrek, as cited in Sgroi (1988), view sexual acting-out behaviors as a solid indication that a youngster is, or has been, sexually exploited. Finkelhor and Browne (1985) note that children who have been sexually traumatized exhibit confused sexual values and ethics. They are unclear about the role of sexuality in intimate relationships and exhibit behaviors deviant from the norm.

ABSENCE OF ANTICIPATORY GUILT

A second form of superego dysfunction identified by Redl and Wineman (1957) is the "inadequacy of the signal function." This is defined as an absence of anticipatory guilt prior to action, although guilty feelings do emerge once the "dirty deed" is done. This may well replicate the sexually abusive situation. The perpetrator's behavior is more compelling than his or her desire or ability to control it. Some child molesters experience guilt after the fact and may become apologetic, offering promises to abstain from such behavior in the future. Generally, however, the abuse continues as do the broken promises to stop it. For the sexually molested child in this situation, the role that is modelled is one in which the adult lacks the ability to foresee the emotional consequences of his or her acts. Therefore, if the child identifies with this adult, the function of being able to anticipate guilt may never become established as part of his or her superego.

FAULTY IDENTIFICATIONS

One of the most severe forms of superego disturbance—the third form identified by Redl and Wineman (1957)—is based on a series of identifications that are superficial, inadequate, or disrupted in their development. Children with this deficit experience a scarcity of consistent, "good enough" adults with whom to identify. The parental objects have been emotionally or physically absent to such an extent that love, in its richest sense, is not engendered in these youngsters. This mutual love between child and adult is the foundation upon which the process of identification is built. By virtue of its absence, the child becomes faulty in his or her superego development. Sarnoff (1976) believes that children who are missing idealizable objects are, in fact, unable to enter latency.

Superego lacunae, which originate from gaps in the identification process, have the potential to surface in sexually abused children who have been subjected to multiple traumas. These may be youngsters who have had early and frequent disruptions of caretakers. They may have been physically abused by the sexual attacker or by other adults, or sexually exploited by a number of people. It is likely that they felt unprotected and unsupported in their attempts to ward off further assaults. The usual hero worship characteristic in latency-age children is replaced in these youngsters by fears of monsters and demons. Moreover, while latency-age children are generally immersed in stories of heroes and myths through which they inculcate the moral fabric and culture of society, abused youngsters are absorbed by ghoulish tales. As a result, they are unable to utilize myths as a way of developing a cultural identity.

GUILT DISPLACEMENT

The last form of superego malfunction, identified by Redl and Wineman (1957), concerns the attachment of guilty feelings to somewhat benign events, while feeling guilt-free during and/or after deviant acts. Sexually maligned children may not feel guilty about sexual activity with a parent, but instead may displace these feelings onto other relatively harmless occurrences such as failing school tests. It is important to remember that during latency school rules and structure become increasingly significant. However, when a child focuses on school problems as a way of avoiding the external and internal chaos generated by the abuse, their function is undermined. Moreover, this child will be unable to adequately acculturate the school environment.

Lack of Remorse

Also included in the fourth category of superego pathology is the youngster's inability to feel guilt if an experience does not have a direct connection to the parent. Molested children can become so rigid in their superego function that they are unable to extract or generalize morality or feelings of conscience to anyone or anything that does not specifically involve the parental object. In this type of disturbance, we see delinquency without remorse. Paradoxically, following the parental dictums to the letter becomes the youngster's modus operandi preventing him or her from autonomous development.

RIGID SUPEREGO

Another form of superego disturbance involves the "overactive" execution of its control. This form of superego dysfunction, which has been traditionally thought of as the neurotic or anxiety disorder, renders the ego ineffectual in moderating between the superego and id demands. The autonomous functioning of the ego is eliminated and its execution is purely contingent upon the superego's whims. In this situation, the superego develops an idealized code of behavior and set of values in which the expression of the sexual and aggressive impulses is strictly forbidden. The constraints are so rigid that psychic health is sacrificed in the process (A. Freud, 1966). Sexually misused latency children may be unable to deploy developmentally appropriate activities to discharge their drives. These children cannot play or utilize fantasy or other subliminatory maneuvers in a satisfactory manner. Often children suffering from this disorder appear lethargic, exhibit signs of anhedonia, and generally lack the spark of childhood.

The superego generally exerts its control by creating guilt and regulating self-esteem. With the rigidified standards discussed above, generating positive feelings towards the self becomes a virtually impossible task as the models are set unrealistically. The demands placed on latency-age children are great. They are measured, and more important they measure themselves against their abilities to produce. Self-esteem is intricately interwoven into how they see themselves within this context. However, children who have been traumatized never meet their internal expectations and chronically suffer from low self-esteem. This prevents these children from experiencing themselves as adequate members of their peer networks.

The projective drawings on the following pages will illustrate the problems that sexually abused youngsters have in the adequate development of superego.

CASE STUDY ANALYSIS OF DRAWINGS

Ginger

Seven-year-old Ginger is one of five siblings. The next to youngest child, she has two brothers, one 11 and one 14, a 13-year-old sister, and an infant sister of 12 months. When Ginger was 3 years old, a male neighbor began to sexually abuse her. It was not until she was 7, however, that she revealed the exploitation. She had been exposed to the perpetrator's naked body, had engaged in mutual fondling, and had participated in oral sex and vaginal intercourse. Unfortunately, this defilement was not the family's only problem. Ginger's mother, Nina, had been chronically battered by her husband, Ginger's father, an active alcoholic. Being victimized was not new to Nina. As a child-victim of sexual abuse perpetrated by her own father, it was all the more painful for Nina to learn that two of her children, Ginger and her 11-year-old son, had both fallen victim to sexual molestation. This family is the epitomy of the upper-middle-class with their financial success and community involvement. However, like other dysfunctional families, their secrets are hidden behind closed doors.

Unlike her family, Ginger does not present us with the façade of a perfect home (Plate 46). In her House Drawing, there are no windows, no door, no path.

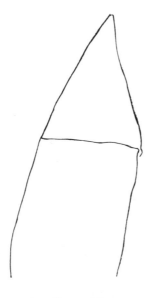

PLATE 46.

Instead, she draws a house devoid of the basic details. She complies with the family dictate of keeping things under wraps to an extreme. She allows no entrance, no exit to her house. Despite Ginger's acknowledgment in the PDI that "the house needs windows and a door to look out and get out," her parental demands have been internalized, albeit with conflict. She complies with the superego demand to keep things inside, yet she verbally expresses her longing for a means to escape her internal prison.

There is evidence that Ginger has developed a rigid superego that is both overcontrolling and punitive. Her strong need to regulate her impulses through superego control is projected through the absence of arms and hands in the Person Drawing in Plate 47. As Hammer (1980) states, "hands and arms are the parts of the human body that 'do things,' establish contact (shake hands), punish or defend" (p. 99). Moreover, the particular body part that is excluded indicates a prohibition regarding its purpose (Kelley, 1984). Therefore, we can conclude that Ginger feels prohibited from acting on her needs. This is a child who is clearly ruled by a superego that overpowers her ego and does not permit a balance between control and action.

In her Person Drawing (Plate 47), the enlarged ears portray a hypersensitivity to criticism (Machover, 1980), which is most likely a projection of Ginger's own negative feelings about herself. These negative thoughts are another means that Ginger uses to control herself. This overregulation is also poignantly reflected by the boxlike structure around the figure's head, the seat of thoughts. Ginger literally attempts to keep the inside in. This is further reflected in the PDI, in which she was unable to suggest a story for either drawing. Unable to fantasize an imaginary tale, she displays yet another component of a rigid superego. This rigidified superego structure functions to inhibit Ginger's ability to adequately enter latency.

PLATE 47.

James

Ten-year-old James, whose ego disturbances were presented in the previous chapter (Plates 30 and 31, pp. 66–67), also manifests problems in his superego. Unfortunately, the physical abuse by his mother and the sexual abuse he was subjected to at the hands of his neighbors have had widespread implications in terms of his overall development. Plate 48 is filled with symbols depicting James's feelings of low self-esteem. These negative feelings are punitive instruments of the superego, indicating that he is not measuring up to his ego ideal.

We are struck by the 2-inch size of James's Person Drawing. Koppitz (1968) identifies a figure of 2 inches or less as an indicator of the artist's emotional disturbance. Di Leo (1973) notes that a youngster employs size to communicate an individual's significance and the regard in which he or she is held. Since the Person Drawing is an inner self-portrait, this figure reflects James's low self-esteem. His presentation illustrates his feeling of "smallness" in relation to the environment. This is further confirmed by the tiny shoulders, which represent James's feelings of inferiority (Jolles, 1971). Another indication of his insecure and inadequate feelings is seen in the low placement of the figure on the page (Mursell, 1969). It is as if he retreats to the lower part of the page instead of putting himself in center stage where he is important. His superego is attempting to control James by telling him he is a bad and unworthy person.

PLATE 48.

Another way in which James's superego is regulating his impulses is through pathological guilt. We see this manifested by the heavily shaded arms. Machover (1980) hypothesized that this treatment represents guilt regarding sexual and aggressive impulses. We fear that this may be a signal that James is frightened of his own aggressive tendencies and of his potential identification with the delinquent values of his abusers.

In fact, his aggression broke through in the PDI when he said that the figure's (Plate 48) parents are dead. "His father died in the war and his mother died of cancer." These comments represent his inner rage at his parents. However, he exerts some control because he said that the figure also wants to die. By this statement James conveys his understanding that there is punishment for his lethal wishes. We also suspect that James is afraid of his wanton sexual impulses as presented by the dark line quality of the belt in Plate 48. This emphasis, which represents sexual preoccupation (Ogdon, 1977), coupled with the shaded arms tells us that James is in danger of identifying with the aggressor and possibly acting on his impulses.

Alice

Six-year-old Alice, whose ego dysfunctions were also discussed earlier (pp. 54–55), displays superego problems in her drawing of a tree (Plate 49). A scribbled crown, as discussed in Chapter 3, represents confused thinking. Koch (1952) also interprets this crown presentation as an indication of the artist's muddled values. We conjecture that Alice is exhibiting signs of a faulty identification process. Those closest to her betrayed her at an early age. As such, she had a paucity of idealizable objects to internalize and from which to develop socially appropriate values. As a result, Alice apparently was unable to develop clarity as to what was right and what was wrong. We refer the reader back to Plate 18 (p. 55), in which Alice drew a buglike monster. This figure represents her inability to identify with heroes and "good guys" and, instead, indicates her propensity to identify and be preoccupied with demons and "bad guys." The potential is great for Alice to be drawn towards delinquent members of society and inculcate asocial mores.

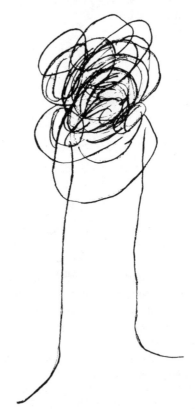

PLATE 49.

Judith

To remind the reader, 7-year-old Judith was sexually abused for many years by a male neighbor. Plates 50, 51, and 52 communicate the effect of life events upon Judith's superego. The weather vane placed on the house (Plate 50) is an unusual, although not bizarre, inclusion. It suggests that this youngster is literally looking to find the way the wind is blowing. A child has generally been able to internalize the parental dictums by age 7 and does not need to look for the "right way." However, Judith is the daughter of a thought-disordered mother who was unable to communicate moral values consistently. This, coupled with the sexual abuse she experienced, further interrupted Judith's superego development.

As such, the weather vane suggests that Judith looks outside of herself for direction, for she is confused about societal mores and, consequently, about her own values. On the positive side, the presence of this weather vane alerts the viewer that Judith is interested in being socially appropriate and accepted by others. The large hands drawn on figures in Plates 50 and 51 connote her concern that she is not socially adept and, in fact, feels quite inadequate in this area (Jolles, 1971).

This may partially be related to secrets Judith feels compelled to keep. The House, like other projective drawings, is really an inner self-portrait. We ask the reader to observe the window on the first floor to the right of the door (Plate 50). The shade on this window is drawn closed. This gives us a clue that Judith needs to hide and cover over "things" within. A further tip about what she needs to conceal is provided through the hair treatment on both figures. The heavily shaded hair on the male figure (Plate 51) and the tightly curled and scribbled hair on the female figure (Plate 52) convey Judith's anxiety about her own thoughts (Jolles, 1971) and possible memories.

However, there is evidence that Judith is trying to prevent these thoughts from becoming conscious. The very well-defined and darkened hair on the male figure denotes her attempt to "cap" these thoughts and constrain them. The female figure also reflects her bid at control. The hair is gathered, held in place, and forcibly restrained by barrettes, which are symbolic representations of a person's struggle to control bodily impulses (Hammer, 1980).

These attempts at constraint are not the well-balanced ego controls that modulate between id and superego. Rather, they are punitive superego measures deployed to punish the child for having bad thoughts. Despite the fact that Judith may not have adequately developed a sense of right and wrong and is probably confused about her own responsibility regarding the abuse, she nevertheless has internalized some sense of propriety. There is a suggestion that Judith feels both culpable and helpless. The outstretched arms and hands on the female figure seem to be crying out for help and assistance. Yet the large hands, weighing down the arms, are unable to fend for themselves.

Unfortunately, Judith sees herself as "the bad one" and feels guilty. We see this evident in the handling of the barrette through which her superego strikes out. The barrette on the left side of the face not only constrains the hair, but looks as if it is piercing the jaw of this helpless girl. It is sadly reminiscent of the way the perpetrator's penis forcibly penetrated Judith.

PLATE 50.

PLATE 51.

PLATE 52.

We see Judith's concern around male genitalia represented in the male figure (Plate 51). The shorts are heavily outlined, as is the zipper. This emphasis of the margins of the trunks and zipper reflects "strong body consciousness with conflict in regard to the concealment and the exhibition of the [male] body" (Machover, 1980, p. 114). We thus note Judith's ambivalence about the abuse. She is unsure whether she wants to cover or reveal the male body.

These mixed feelings add to Judith's guilt and sense of culpability for the abuse. In her PDI in response to the instruction to draw a person of the opposite sex, she said, "Don't say that word sex. . . . Do you know what happened to me? I got raped. . . . That word gets me embarrassed." These feelings of shame, humiliation, responsibility, and guilt over the satisfaction derived from the abusive relationship are similar to those that many sexually misused youngsters experience. These emotions lead to a complicated and confused superego structure, which leaves these youngsters with mixed values about right and wrong, and specifically with a perplexed sense of their own responsibility and culpability.

Henry

Henry is the product of a multiproblem family, who lives in a low-income inner-city slum. Abuse, poverty, and lack of emotional and financial resources are woven into his psychological fabric. The abuse in his family began before he was born. His father battered his mother during her pregnancy, kicking her in the stomach and chronically assaulting her. Remarkably, the pregnancy was full-term, with no complications either during labor or delivery. All of Henry's developmental milestones were within the normal range.

As a result of the chronic and severe battering, the mother separated from the father when Henry was about 1 year old. There has been little contact between Henry and his alcoholic father since that time. Once his father moved out of the house, Henry's mother moved the child into the parental bed. Sleeping with his mother has been, to some extent, a stimulating experience to him. Over the ensuing years, Henry has had an inconsistent relationship with his mother. He has been continually beaten by her, frequently without rhyme or reason. Yet he continued to sleep in her bed until one month before the projective tests were administered. This change in his sleeping arrangements resulted from his disclosure in therapy that he was sexually abused by a male teenage neighbor. Medical examination revealed scarring to the anal tissues, confirming that he was anally sodomized.

Henry's family had already begun services at a local abuse prevention center several months before the disclosure. The mother had sought help after Henry—as described by his mother—became "wild," pulled a knife on his 7-year-old sister, lit fire to the bathroom curtains, and became totally unmanageable at home. To mitigate against inadequate models, and to provide indealizable objects, the agency enrolled Henry in a local day-care center. The center has reported that Henry hits other youngsters and has great difficulty following directions.

Not surprisingly, the sexual abuse has put this already vulnerable child in an insufferable position. He has few inner assets to meet a largely unsupportive

PLATE 53.

and hostile environment; his drawings reflect this. His Tree Drawing (Plate 53) is peculiarly unrecognizable as a tree and contains an enclosure. These features are frequently drawn by sexually molested youngsters (Cohen & Cox, 1989). His sketches of both a person and a person of the opposite sex (Plates 54 and 55 respectively) leave no doubt in the viewer's eye that these are monsters. If there is a question, Henry tells us in the PDI that they are, in fact, "monsters." The demons from the outside have turned into monsters on the inside. These ghoulish figures now occupy Henry's inner life. They suggest that his inner tensions are too strong and that he is unable to use his ego resources for constructive solutions to everyday problems.

The hair in Plates 54 and 55, emphasized through the long and wild display, connotes that Henry indulges his impulses to immediate gratification (Shneidman, 1958). We know that up to this time Henry's surroundings have reinforced acting out. His mother is unable to provide the structure or values he so desperately needs, for she often responds to his actions with her own violent outbursts. Her behavior, thereby, models impulsive responses. Complicating this further is the unpredictable and repeatedly violent anal penetration to which he was recently victim. This provided another model of acting out as the modus operandi.

Both Person Drawings symbolically project Henry's identification with "the bad guys" and show that he is not using the typical latency-age heroes to help him develop appropriate cultural values. It seems, actually, that Henry has no values. However, the monster figures contradict this impression. The reality is that he has internalized distorted images in order to come to terms with his physical and sexual abuse. He has identified with the aggressor. His ego ideal

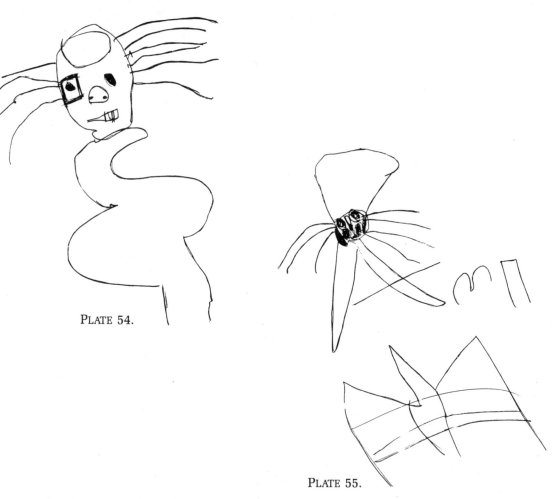

PLATE 54.

PLATE 55.

has become antisocial, hostile, and abusive. Moreover, his self-esteem seems to be regulated by his capacity to be as tough as his abusers.

Yet it would be impossible for Henry to measure up to this ideal. He has been incapable of defending himself against either his mother or the perpetrator. This leaves him feeling totally inadequate. The grotesque images tell us that Henry is sorely lacking positive self-esteem. The hole in the head and the blackened eye (Plate 54) suggest his sense of feeling damaged and "no good." How positive could he feel about himself with a hole in his head? Doesn't it suggest that he feels stupid, as if he had no brains?

Jack

Six-year-old Jack was presented in Chapter 3 (p. 58). His House Drawing (Plate 21) depicted his problems in cognitive development as well as his tendency to isolate his affect. In Plates 56, 57, and 58 are projected indices of the sexual exploitation. We note the thinning of the hair at the crown on all the figures, the monsterlike person in Plate 58 (Cohen & Cox, 1989). Unquestionably, the sexual abuse significantly impacted on the formation of Jack's superego. Because of his parents' inadequacies, he experienced gaps in the process of his early identifications. His father sexually abused him; his mother did not protect him. This has resulted in the development of a superego disturbance that Redl and Wineman (1957) call "faulty identifica-

PLATE 56.

PLATE 57.

Brother
3

Sister
(7)

Jack
5

dad

mom

PLATE 58.

tions." Jack's Tree Drawing (Plate 56), which is bizarre and almost unrecognizable, is another marker of probable sexual abuse (Cohen & Cox, 1989). Moreover, the scribbled, disorganized crown (Plate 56) is indicative of Jack's confused thinking and value structure and his resulting muddle about how to properly behave (Koch, 1952).

Before we look further at the drawings, let us remind the reader that objects on the left side of the page are believed to reflect concerns about the past (Jolles, 1971; Ogdon, 1977). Furthermore, parts of a drawing that are placed on the left side may also relate to the past (Wohl & Kaufman, 1985). Note the left side of the root structure of Jack's Tree Drawing. It is disconnected from the trunk, while the right side shows a firm connection to it through a dark and continuous line. The source of Jack's confused values is suggested by this root treatment.

Jack's mother tried to teach him acceptable standards of behavior (although she never protected him), while his father, through the sexual defilement, modelled a bastardization of morals. The authors hypothesize that the differential handling of the tree roots represents the influence of both parents on his superego. Jack's broken connection to his father (his father has moved out of state and has little contact with Jack) and his father's value structure are reflected by the root treatment on the left; his ongoing attachment to his mother is seen in the right root treatment. Although Jack's internalization of his father is formidable, it is nonetheless cut off, while his mother's influence is ever present. Although Jack is physically disconnected from his father, we notice that he has placed himself beside his father in the KFD (Plate 57). Their arms are looped together. As much as Jack may try to detach from his father, he is unable to shake his presence.

Jack has incorporated some of his father's values especially around sexuality and sexual acting out. There are a number of sexual symbols and innuendos in the drawings and in the PDI. In the Tree Drawing (Plate 56) there is a breast protruding from the left side of the crown; the father in the KFD (Plate 57) has a huge, piercing penis hanging between his legs. When one keeps in mind that Jack was anally penetrated by his father, the youngster's comments in the PDI are poignant. In response to the question, "What is the best part of the tree?" he answers "The stump. It holds in real good. . . . It stays in real tight." The combination of the sexualized drawing items, Jack's comments in the PDI, and his observed behavior (he has engaged in cunnilingus with his sister) leads us to conclude that Jack is identifying with his father, although he remains confused and probably guilt-ridden. The absence of hands on the figures may be indicative of this guilt (Ogdon, 1977). While it is not necessarily expected that a 6-year-old will draw hands (Koppitz, 1968), we see in Plate 58 that Jack has included one hand and is therefore capable of drawing this body part.

Jessica

Jessica, who was sexually abused by her grandfather, was discussed in Chapter 3 (see Plate 22, p. 59) as having difficulty in logical thinking. The authors also stated that she utilizes considerable energy to contain her libidinal drives. Jessica's grandfather confessed to the abuse after she disclosed it to her mother. Had her grandfather not admitted to the molestation, Jessica's Person Drawing, Person of the Opposite Sex Drawing, and Tree Drawing (Plates 59, 60, and 61 respectively) would raise our suspicions as they are littered with indices of her sexual abuse.

The hole in the tree trunk (Plate 61) alerts us to the probability that Jessica has been traumatized. In her drawing of the person (Plate 59), the differential treatment of the arms, the head over one-quarter of the size of the figure (Blain, Bergner, Lewis, & Goldstein, 1981), and the presence of extraneous circles (Sidun & Rosenthal, 1987) are all suggestive of sexual abuse. This implication is further confirmed by the monsterlike male figure (Plate 60), with its unusual mouth treatment (Cohen & Phelps, 1985), the absence of hands, the heavy lines, the presence of extraneous circles again (Sidun & Rosenthal, 1987), and the noticeable difference in the size of the arms. We also note that there is no way of determining the male from the female figure. Kelley (1985) cites this as a likely indicator of sexual trauma.

The sexual abuse that was forced upon 10-year-old Jessica has taken its toll on her superego functions. These three drawings reflect a rigid superego in which she attempts to utilize an idealized standard of behavior, while denying expression of any sexual or aggressive drives. A thick, elongated neck is present on both the male and female figures. This signifies Jessica's excessive concern with morals (Machover, 1980). In addition, the tree is drawn in a very stereotypical manner. This also conveys her overinvestment in convention (Koch, 1952). The expression of her rigid superego underscores the picture presented by Jessica's House Drawing (Plate 22), where she offered a "proper" show of what should be. This is particularly problematic for a latency-age child, as this type of superego dysfunction results in the inability to utilize spontaneous play and to take pleasure in activities. This constraint is reflected in the crown of her Tree Drawing (Plate 61), where her tendency to contain and restrain is depicted.

PLATE 59.   PLATE 60.

PLATE 61.

Jan

Jan, who is 8 and a half years old, is a pretty blue-eyed blond-haired young-ster. Her voice and body gestures are brimming with coquettish and flirta-tious mannerisms. Jan's working-class family consists of herself, her mother, father, older brother, and a paternal older female cousin who has lived with the family for seven years. All three children were sexually abused by their maternal grandfather, who confessed upon the youngsters' disclosures. The ongoing abuse involved mutual fondling, cunnilingus, and attempted penetra-tion. The grandfather would typically send two children out on an errand before molesting the third child. He would frequently nap with the would-be victim. The children reported that when alone with him individually, they would sometimes awaken to find their grandfather on top of them.

At the time the abuse was disclosed, Jan manifested a number of Post-Traumatic Stress Disorder symptoms, as well as bedwetting, frequent headaches, separation anxiety, a drop in school performance, talking aloud in her sleep, and a repetitive nightmare about a hand emerging and grabbing her. Hints of the sexual abuse Jan experienced are seen in the House Drawing in the differential treatment of one window (Cohen & Phelps, 1985) and in the inclusion of extraneous circles (Sidun & Rosenthal, 1987) (Plate 62). In the Person of the Opposite Sex Drawing (Plate 63) the head is over one-quarter of the size of the total figure, an exaggeration further indicating abuse (Blain, Bergner, Lewis, & Goldstein, 1981).

Psychological evaluation of Jan revealed her overconcern with aggression and physical vulnerability. In response to the Rorschach Test, she saw hands with blood gushing out, which was interpreted to represent her anxiety about

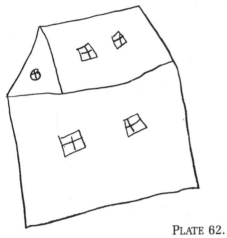

PLATE 62.

PLATE 63.

PLATE 64.

PLATE 65.

PLATE 66.

digital penetration or masturbatory experiences. In addition, the tests uncovered that Jan was afraid of feeling out of control and of being overwhelmed by external forces.

Interestingly, in the PDI to Jan's House Drawing (Plate 62) she stated "there was a house, hit by a hurricane and the house was in terrible shape. People in it got hurt . . . the wind came and the house went apart. The pool in the backyard and water came out and [there] was a hole." This vivid description conveys the devastating effect the sexual abuse had upon Jan and her family. The sexual assaults have, in fact, literally split the family apart.

Her dramatic story also alerts the interpreter to Jan's sense of impulses running wild. We see this symbolically presented by the overflowing pool (Plate 62), as well as by the protrusions in the heads of the figures in Plates 64 and 65. In Jan's HFD (Plate 64), we note a crossed-out figure to the left of the girl. Burns and Kaufman (1972) recognize an "X" as typically drawn by children inhibited by a strong superego. The X is a metaphor embodying a force and a counterforce. We suspect that Jan is struggling to eradicate her very strong sexual and aggressive impulses. We wonder if Jan also witnessed the sexual molestation of the other two children, for the large hollow eyes seen in Plates 63 and 64 suggest guilt regarding voyeuristic tendencies (Jolles, 1971).

Jan's self-esteem has also been damaged. The diminutive dimensions of both the tree (Plate 66) and the female human figure (Plate 64) are readily noticeable. These unusually small drawings suggest her discontentment with herself and her low self-esteem (Di Leo, 1973; Koppitz, 1968). Further confirmation of these negative feelings are seen in the finger treatment (Plates 63 and 64). The tiny hands and missing fingers combine to paint a picture of child who feels inadequate and insecure (Machover, 1980). Note the bony shoulders on the female figure (Plate 64). The special treatment of this body part is interpreted as an expression of the need for physical power (Ogdon, 1977). The skinny shoulders mirror Jan's feelings of weakness and self-doubt.

Her sense of insecurity is further highlighted by the ground line in the KFD (Plate 65). As Burns and Kaufman state, "When our world seems unstable so that we might tumble over, we stabilize it with a firm foundation . . . lining at the bottom" (1972, p. 123). The presence of a line at the top of a drawing may represent the environment as filled with darkness and worry (Burns & Kaufman, 1972). These two lines also serve to encapsulate this sexually abused family as if to underline the isolation that they have experienced.

Jane

Ten-year-old Jane's spontaneous Person Drawing, which was presented earlier (Plate 10, p. 49), depicted the effects that one incident of sexual abuse appeared to have upon her ego. In late latency, sexual impulses are normally quiet and just beginning to bud. However, Jane's were prematurely and inappropriately aroused by her father's traumatic sexual acting out. Psychological and psychiatric evaluations, as well as ongoing clinical appraisals, determined that Jane was manifesting symptoms consistent with Post-Traumatic Stress Disorder. These characteristics can be transient, especially with the aid of psychotherapy. However, the HFD (Plate 67), the Person of the Opposite Sex Drawing (Plate 68), and the House Drawing (Plate 69) provide the interpreter with information about her superego development, which is more alarming because these effects may be more lasting.

Jane's sexual and aggressive impulses are breaking through in each drawing presented. In the female figure (Plate 67), the sexualized neckline and the tightly pulled-in waist, giving a corsetlike appearance, suggest her tenuous control over her bodily impulses (Machover, 1980). More obvious, and also confusing to the observer, are the two elongated protrusions, one from each side of the waist. Do these represent the ends of a bow tied in the back, or are they without rational description? Although we do not have the answer to these quandaries, there is little question that their presence represents either a breakthrough of impulses or an extreme attempt at controlling them.

The large hands (Plate 67) (Di Leo, 1973) and the sharp pointed blades of grass framing the House Drawing (Plate 69) alert us to Jane's potential problems with anger. Although Jane's overt behavior is not currently aggressive or hostile, we can see from the drawings that these issues exist. It is likely that they are manifested through her reported nightmares and current eating difficulties. Hints of the source of her aggression are reflected in her representation of a male (Plate 68). He bears exposed teeth, which suggest aggressive acting out (Koppitz, 1968).

Di Leo (1973) notes that portrayal of a figure can depict a youngster's feelings towards that individual. It seems that this picture is symbolic of Jane's fear of male aggression. The suggestion of her trepidation about male sexuality is seen through the shaded hair (Urban, 1963), the presence of the goatee (Buck, 1981), and the hidden hands (Jolles, 1971). In addition, a dropped waist,

PLATE 67.

PLATE 68.

PLATE 69.

such as on this figure, connotes sexual tensions (Machover, 1980) and is yet another indication of Jane's concerns about male sexuality.

The pressuring sexual and aggressive impulses Jane experiences have culminated in the development of compensatory rigid superego controls. The rulerlike lines delineating the walls of the house, windows, windowpanes, door, and tree (Plate 69) suggest her attempt to precisely define parameters. The belt and shoelaces on the man (Plate 68) are further evidence of Jane's efforts to control aggressive and sexual drives. The man's pocket-covered hands tell us about the presence of guilty feelings (Ogdon, 1977). When we look at the female figure (Plate 67) our eyes catch the paper-doll-like dress held in front of the body. Like the face mask discussed in Chapter 3 that covered the "real self," this strangely shaped dress serves to cloak bodily drives. Again, we see an example of how Jane's superego is pressuring to flatten and squelch what may be hidden underneath. We wonder what felt ugliness Jane is trying to control and hide.

Another superego deficit is in Jane's self-esteem. Ogdon (1977) suggests that a tip-toe stance conveys feelings of inadequacy. We note that the woman seems to be tenuously balanced on the edge of her toes and appears to be struggling to maintain her balance. She is not surefooted and is thereby reflecting her feeling of incompetence. The oversized dress is a further indication of her low self-esteem. It is as if she feels too small to adequately fill out her clothes. Perhaps she does not measure up to her own expectations. This 10-year-old child in fact still feels a lot like a little girl. The demure animal peeking out of the tree (Plate 69) is indicative of Jane's desire to return once again to the safe security of the womb (Jolles, 1971).

CONCLUSION

Sexual molestation of latency children ruthlessly assaults their superego, with the resulting aberrations taking a variety of forms. Youngsters may develop faulty identifications or feel guilty about relatively inconsequential events. They may develop a rigid superego or be unable to feel remorse. Like other latency-age achievements, the enhancement of the superego is a paramount goal, but sexually abused youngsters fail to adequately identify with both individual models and the society at large. They become largely incapable of acculturating societal mores.

Therefore, these children are undermined in their ability to master age-appropriate superego tasks. They are bereft and not prepared to move into adolescence. Moreover, they are inadequately equipped with the moral fabric and internal structure to prepare them for satisfying and productive functioning as they move through adolescence into adulthood.

CHAPTER 5

THE INCESTUOUS FAMILY'S INFLUENCE ON THE DEVELOPMENT OF OBJECT RELATIONS DURING LATENCY

As stated earlier, one of the major tasks for latency-age children is the expansion of their relationships beyond those of the nuclear family. Although the foundation for object relations are in place by this period, there is an epigenetic progression in its future development. The way by which a family allows the latency-age youngster to venture forth creates a cast by which interactions are hereafter set. Moreover, this pattern is inextricably hinged to the dynamics of the family system.

A healthy family supports the growth and development of its members. Integral to this is a firm set of boundaries that contains a degree of permeability at the same time. New information is welcomed and the family is open to outside influences. This is the basis of an open family system (Hoffman, 1981). The unit's basic shape, structure, and integrity remain firm; the roles and intergenerational boundaries remain fixed. Yet, the growing child is encouraged to bring his or her own unique contributions to the family, thereby impacting upon the entire system. Differences between members are not only tolerated, but they are accepted and fostered. Concomitantly, a sense of familial sameness and belonging are promoted. These delicate balances, which continually challenge the system, are faulty in an incestuous family to a greater or lesser degree. Moreover, it is often because they are out of sync that an incestuous relationship is able to begin. Thereafter, it is these, as well as other family dynamics, that inevitably support its perpetuation.

Many ingredients of the growing child's basic personality are mutilated as a result of interactions in a disturbed family system. In particular, the object relations of the sexually abused child become deformed (Brothers, 1982). Keep in mind that latency is the period during which youngsters are normatively venturing out into the world, taking what they have learned about relating to others and generalizing this to the environment at large. Children gradually move away from the solitary influence of the nuclear family and struggle to integrate the values of the larger society into the framework of those previously internalized from their parents. For child-victims of incest, this becomes an arduous task. Trapped within the web of the dysfunctional family, these children may be unable to extricate themselves sufficiently to integrate the new experiences they have had with others. They may also misinterpret interactions, viewing them through the distorted lens of the abusive familial paradigm.

THE CHARACTERISTICS OF THE INCESTUOUS FAMILY

Our clinical experience, which is supported by the literature (Cohen, 1983; Everstine & Everstine, 1989; Hillman & Solek-Tefft, 1988), has led us to conclude that there are some specific patterns and characteristics typical to the incestuous family. According to Finkelhor (1986), a number of factors have a high correlation to sexual abuse. These include parental absence and unavailability, conflict between the parents, the presence of a stepfather, and the child's poor parental relationships (specifically with the mother). In addition, are the environmental stressors that frequently precipitate aberrant sexual behavior. These strains may include job loss, and the subsequent forfeiture of status, severe parental illness, parental death or desertion, and/or immigration to a new country. It is important to understand that severe stress limits one's ability to make sound decisions and to control improper inclinations. Incest, in fact, has been viewed (MacFarlane et al., 1986) as just such a symptom in a family that is pervasively anguished. It is this component of stress when combined with the unfortunate mix of character (which we will discuss below) that leads to a high-risk potential for incestuous behavior.

The characteristics common in incestuous families are found also in functional families (Maltz & Holman, 1987). However, it is the configuration of a number of these attributes that forms the basis on which an incestuous relationship is built. It is essential to realize that the incestuous family gestalt is not necessarily the same for each family. Albeit, certain common denominators exist. Most incestuous families appear, to the casual observer, to be well-adjusted, well-functioning, and nurturing child-centered units. The fathers, in fact, seem to be "family men," highly invested in their family unit. Frequently, both the children and parents act as if they feel capable and adept. Often a façade of competence is presented, giving the illusion that the members are comfortable in their family roles. Closer observation reveals another reality.

Roles

A primary problem in sexually exploitive families is that role delineations are confused and garbled. There is a dysfunctional fluidity between the role of parent and child. Selected youngsters often become parentified and then, at the whim of the adult, are relegated back to the child position. For the abused youngsters, this becomes immensely confusing. Their place in the world and where they fit in become muddled.

This weak structure in role definition represents a more generalized problem in which diffuse boundaries exist between members, and the family is enmeshed. This is manifested by the members' oblivion to each other's separateness, low toleration for any differences, and total disregard for psychological and physical privacy (members may walk in and out of the bathroom regardless of who may be in there). Possessions are not respected as owned by another. Moreover, there is a customary "open-door" policy in the family in which closed doors are literally not tolerated and, in some cases, are even physically removed.

Separation Anxiety

There is a primitive terror in the incestuous family in relation to its dissolution. The family suffers from what could be considered a familial "Separation Anxiety Disorder." The members are frequently unable to tolerate being apart from the others, for they each feel they are not whole without the presence of everyone. In other words, the sense of self is pathologically tied to each and every family member. The individuals are incapable of functioning independently and use each other to fill in gaps of the self and the self functions. An experience of emptiness and incompleteness shrouds each family member, leaving him or her to feel like an emotional amputee when the potential loss of another is feared.

Collusion

Members of sexually abusing families also tend to collude, either consciously or unconsciously, to perpetuate and to preserve the abuse. By so doing, they maintain a distorted sense of familial integrity. Although the sexual violation is performed by an abusive individual, it often has the unspoken, or unconscious, support of the nonoffending members. This conspiracy serves to preserve the continuity of the family. Cohen (1983), in fact, believes that this complicity is preserved in order to defend against family disintegration and fragmentation. It is almost as if one child is unconsciously being offered in sacrifice to "save" the family.

Dependence vs. Independence

Understanding the balance of dependence versus independence in the incestuous family is fundamental to understanding its functioning. Each individual, to a greater or lesser degree, surrenders his or her autonomy for both personal and familial survival. Possessing a long history of deprivation, each deeply needy member is, in effect, looking for the mother who was never available (Geiser, 1979). This object hunger results in the forfeiture of the self in a desperate hope that basic nurturance will be forthcoming. An example of this is the mother's abdication of her own independence for need satisfaction, as she develops an ever-increasing dependency upon her child. This often occurs when the mother's early experiences with her family of origin predispose her to casting one of her youngsters into an incestuous relationship with her husband.

The Mother's Relationship to Her Incestuously Abused Child

Mothers in families where the husband* is the abuser frequently have intergenerational separation difficulties that are demonstrated by their inability to move either physically or psychologically away from their own mothers. Even as adults, they tend to obsess about gaining maternal approval and acceptance, which is never forthcoming. This is because an unconscious pattern was created in these women in childhood when their own mothers viewed them as worthless, and any sign of their own emotional health or independence was not tolerated.

According to Kaufman, Peck, and Tagiuri (1954), the next generation sees a recurrence of this pattern. An unconsciously selected daughter is cast into the role of the maternal grandmother by the mother. Although the mother may give this child excellent physical care, she, nonetheless, displaces repressed and hostile impulses meant for the maternal grandmother onto her. The youngster is given age-inappropriate responsibilities which cause the child to be overtaxed. In time, the youngster grows hostile towards her mother, replicating the earlier animosity projected by the maternal grandmother onto the mother.

With the ever-increasing burden of responsibilities of caring for younger siblings and of household duties, Kaufman, Peck and Tagiuri (1954) conclude that such girls become increasingly directive and independent, eventually reversing roles with their mothers. Often fuelled by the mother's emotional and sexual desertion of their husbands, the process culminates with the daughter's assuming wifely duties, including sexual activities with their fathers. Maltz and Holman (1987), in referring to this operation, coined the phrase "executive child" for this youngster whose responsibilities are enormous. Over time, the mothers grow resentful towards these daughters, experiencing them as bossy, antagonistic, excessively independent, and (upon disclosure) at fault for the incest.

This results in the emotional abandonment of this youngster by her mother in the service of the mother's unconscious needs. The daughter is then placed in the same position as her mother, desperately longing for maternal approval and nurturance. The sexually abusive cycle is once again begun and the stage is set for reenactment in the next generation.

The Father's Relationship to His Incestuously Abused Child

The control that the father generally assumes emanates not from a place of strength, but conversely from a pervasive feeling of inadequacy, vulnerability,

---

*As this is the most common scenario, it is the one we will concentrate on. However, if the mother is the sexually exploitive adult, the concepts are applicable in reverse. Sibling incest involves another set of dynamics, which will not be dealt with here, but it should be noted that the aftermath of this abuse is also devastating.

and helplessness. As the perpetrator, he selects a child to relate to in substitution for an adult, precisely because he feels incapable of having an intimate adult relationship. The child molestation, according to Groth, Hobson, and Gary (1982), is the father's sexualization of nonsexual needs such as acceptance, enhancement of self-worth, and love.

Problems with Intimacy and Closeness

This powerful configuration demonstrates how very threatening independent functioning is to the life of the sexually abusive family. Kaufman, Peck, and Tagiuri (1954) see not only the mothers as dependent and infantile, but the fathers as well. In addition, Maltz and Holman (1987) comment that neither parent is truly capable of establishing an intimate adult relationship; in order to do so, one must be prepared to commit to another. Such a commitment requires serious concession and negotiation, qualities that are generally absent in these partners.

The inability of parents in incestuous homes to form meaningful, functional adult-to-adult relationships frequently leads to social isolation, another classic symptom of the incestuous family. Members are discouraged from having contact with people outside the family and thereby are seldom able to establish closeness with others. From a structural theory framework (Minuchin, 1974), this can be thought of as a family with "rigid boundaries" built around itself—barriers that inevitably help to protect and to preserve the sexually violating behavior.

Integral to this isolation are secrets that shield from "strangers" the truth about the sexual abuse. In addition, there are intrafamilial secrets that help to maintain pretenses. This, coupled with the family's habitually poor communication, isolates and estranges the members from one another (MacFarlane et al., 1986). Paradoxically, although separation is not tolerated, these concealed facts inevitably build walls between the members. Although these obstructions are translucent, allowing a vague glimmer of truth to emerge slowly, denial is the modus operandi in these households and, as such, protects the individuals against the truth and against the concomitant flood of anxiety.

The reason incestuous families are unable to share true intimacy with one another or with outsiders is that each member is forced into a position of self-absorption. It is this self-absorption that creates a situation fertile for the propagation of the incestuous behavior. Both parents, capable of only pseudointimacy, are basically attuned to themselves. Their marriage can be viewed as an "isolation à deux," in which each partner is protected from the awareness that she or he is unable to establish a mature closeness. In fact, although these couples may appear to outsiders to have a "good marriage" and may even share an active, albeit unsatisfying, sexual life, their pervasive lack of intimacy belies this charade.

Problems with intimacy are played out not only in their role as husband and wife, but also in their role as parents. They are typically insensitive to the needs and wishes of their children, ignoring the youngsters' feelings, moods, and general state of being. They both generalize and project their own emotions onto their offspring and, by so doing, disregard the children.

Locus of Control

Another critical quality found in this pathogenic system is in the locus and distribution of power. Typically, the fathers in these families possess a disproportionate level of authority, although there are also circumstances in which the greater share of power is vested in the mother. This creates a power imbalance and perpetuates a lack of control and autonomy in the other family members. This inequitable distribution of power fosters an environment fertile for abuse and its sequelae. Finkelhor (1986) focuses part of his conceptual framework of incest on the effects sexual exploitation has on the molested child. He concludes that "powerlessness" is a major psychological condition resulting from the assault. Victims are systematically made to feel they have no control over anything in their lives—including their own bodies. In effect, the victims are brainwashed, becoming unable to discriminate between situations that they have the power to change and those that they don't. Eventually, the child-victim is rendered helpless with the father in total control.

Father's Ego Deficits

Fathers have also been found to exhibit many ego deficits that affect their relationships with their sons and/or daughters. Poor judgment is one area identified (Bresee et al., 1986) that is consistent with sexually abusive behavior. Distorted thinking represents another impaired ego function (Maltz & Holman, 1987). These distortions are evident when the fathers excuse their abusive behavior with such explanations as, "Well, she or he liked the sex." The regulation and modulation of affects are difficult for these men. A minor event may trigger a rageful response that is inappropriate for the given situation.

Father's Attempt to Rework His Own Past

Just as the mother, described earlier, uses her daughter to replay the unresolved relationship with her own mother, the perpetrating father uses his child to rework his own unsettled past. This history is saturated with pervasive experiences of humiliation and denigration which threaten his deepest sense of self. The father attempts to fight against his feelings of helplessness by identifying with an aggressor and thereby becoming the victimizer rather than the victim. In this way, he strives to reestablish a much earlier sense of his own worth and power, utilizing a mode of behavior he probably learned from his own family of origin. By so doing, he becomes the abuser and his child may learn to become a helpless victim. Some children, however, will learn to model their father's behavior and instead will use force and power as a way of relating to others.

Father's Impulse Control Problems

Impulse control problems in incestuous homes are particularly noteworthy and universally cited throughout the literature (Bresee, Stearns, Bess, & Packer, 1986; Everstine & Everstine, 1989; Lieske, 1981; Sgroi, 1982). Frequently, the manifestation of these problems is confined to the family, with the father appearing to observers as a highly moral member of the community. However, the impulse difficulties of some fathers may be more pervasive, affecting many areas of functioning, such as the abuse of substances, poor job performance, and brawls with friends. In the family setting, the father's impulse problems are often directed towards the sexually exploited youth, with whom the father is generally unpredictable.

The Intergenerational Effects

In fact, the conduct of both the fathers and mothers in incestuous families reveals the marks of intergenerational scarring. The roles of victim, enabler, and perpetrator are familiar to them. These behaviors, even if uncomfortable, are unconsciously acceptable. The unfortunate reality is that the majority of sexual offenders have themselves been sexually offended (Groth et al., 1982) or have a father who molested others within their childhood household. The mothers, likewise, as noted by Maltz and Holman (1987), were victimized as children and have identified with and incorporated the helplessness they observed in their own mothers. They grew up assuming that being malevolently controlled was an expected and unchallengeable way of life.

The family atmosphere in which the incestuously abused child lives and breathes is filled with the pollutants we have described. The dynamics of the family system and the subtleties consequently engendered serve to poison all of the youngster's future relationships and, as such, severely impact on the ongoing development of object relations during latency.

DEVELOPMENT OF OBJECT RELATIONS

Regardless of the environment in which a youngster grows up, the parental objects perform a variety of functions in helping him or her to adapt. The parents provide models through which the child learns what he or she can expect from others. They furnish a fault-finding inner voice (or superego) which helps to control and otherwise socialize the youngster. Ideally, they help also to soothe the child in periods of anxiety and loneliness (Greenberg & Mitchell, 1983). Children raised in sexually abusive homes of immature adults who are unattuned and unable to providing nourishment, and beyond that in households where children are frequently supposed to furnish a multitude of satisfactions to the parents or older relatives, learn to adapt to this pathological environment. These child-victims then replicate their maladaptive strategies in their relationships outside the home, invariably misreading and misinterpreting the actions of others in their bids to fit them back into their own internal structures.

Love and the Incestuous Relationship

Love is a complex phenomenon between individuals. Between child and parent, or between child and other trusted or older family members, it comprises a multidimensional and intricate interaction permeated with sensations, feelings, and behaviors. According to Arlow (as cited in Buckley, 1986), love is based on fairness to others, the curtailment of aggressive acts, compassion, and "a capacity for positively tinged affective identification with others" (p. 127).

Society places a profound moral worth on love and, as such, the superego guides the actions of the individual to favor his or her loved object. The incestuously abused child's relationship to the perpetrator, although cultivated under the guise of love, does not contain the most basic elements necessary for healthy love either to flourish or to be growth-enhancing. In the sexually abusive family, aggression is often pervasive, lack of compassion is the modus operandi, and empathy is sorely absent. Instead, the abuser's wants and wishes are superimposed upon the innocent youngster. The child desperately needs and wants a reciprocal emotional interaction with the perpetrator. The child's need is so intense that she or he is willing to go to great lengths—and to succumb to so much—to receive it. Yet the molested youngster experiences the abuser's "love" offering with immense anxiety. It is this very need for love that makes the youngster vulnerable and susceptible to misuse, and this need for love ultimately has the potential to devastate him or her when it is mishandled.

Many incestuously abused juveniles have been victim to what Sullivan coined "Malevolent Transformation." Chranowski (1978) explains this concept as the child seeking tenderness from a trusted other and instead receiving constant rejection and/or degradation, hostility then surfaces in its place when the need for gentleness later arises. As he states, the child bites "the hand that one would like to be stroked by tenderly" (p. 405). Eventually, the youngster becomes unable to discern a tender response when one happens and fears and anticipates punishment at any time.

By the same token, the child has learned through the way in which each family member uses one another to maintain each others' stability that the only love that counts is that which involves the surrender of a person's own self. In this vein, the child often continues to seek positive parental responsiveness. However, it is a fruitless search, for, as discussed earlier, the parents are self-involved and unable to provide the understanding reactions for which the youngster hungers. The child interprets this to means he or she is the "bad" one, thereafter, tending to set him or herself up in situations in which he or she is rejected and even scapegoated. Conversely, the child may take these feelings of rejection, utilize the defensive maneuver of reversal to defend against the tremendous anxiety generated, and reject others before they reject him or her.

The World of the Youngster as Defined by Family's Values

It is important to understand that the reality of the latency child's world is predominately defined by his or her family. The child's sense of morality, in particular, is weaved by the tapestry of the family milieu. In an incestuous family, however, there is a bastardization of morals and the youngster's reality becomes dystonic with that of the greater society. Latency children are dependent on the family's and, particularly, on the parents' judgment; as such, when invited or lured into an incestuous relationship, they may be agreeable initially.

However, as child-victims increasingly experience new situations outside of the household, they come to realize the sexual behavior is wrong and, as important, comprehend that it is repugnant to others. As a result, these youngsters often feel self-contempt. Feeling shattered by the betrayal of their family members, they may also lose all sense of trust in them. On the other hand, the youngsters may react to the incest paradoxically by trusting family members and others even more as a way of preserving their faith in the outside world, upon which they are vitally dependent. At the same time, these victims begin to discount their own feelings of self.

The consequences of a parent's, relative's, older sibling's, or trusted caretaker's perverse misuse of a child to fulfill his or her own needs have profound repercussions on the youngster's future object relations. These children may develop an impoverished ability to discriminate between questionable and trustworthy individuals. They may no longer be capable of trusting their own judgments and perceptions about others and thereby find themselves unable to function and relate to others in developmentally appropriate or independent ways. These youngsters may have a desperate need to seek out others to provide clarification and definitions. For example, these victims may be followers, unable to initiate activities and thereby unable to develop this critical latency-age skill. In order to maintain friendships, these children may surrender themselves to please others, replicating the way they forfeit themselves through the sexual abuse. Again, these youngsters are at risk of developing a false self and a pseudomanner of relating to others.

Relationships Beyond the Family

Due to incest in the family, latency-age children's ability to form close attachments is severely impaired. The imbalance of power that is misused and ultimately exploits them, leads to troubled peer and authority relations. Often these children remain outside of relationships, never feeling truly involved. If they identify with the aggressor, they may become bossy and bullying, which creates distant relationships. Conversely, in the course of forming relationships, they may take on the role of rescuer as an attempt to restore a sense of power and belief in themselves. Regardless of the role these victims assume in any relationship, a healthy mutuality is generally lacking.

Another problem sexually abused latency children carry forth from the home is the absence of a clear sense of self, especially in regard to their ego boundaries. These youngsters have been violated in every way imaginable. A normally developing infant feels one with the parent. Through maturation, in a healthy supportive environment, the infant slowly begins to separate and learns where he or she ends and the other begins. The infant is allowed to assert him or herself, and a certain degree of aggression is tolerated. However, exploited children are not permitted autonomy or any expression of power in the abusive encounter. They either remain fused to the perpetrator or, if a previous psychological separation was achieved, they may regress to a lack of differentiation. Healthy ego boundaries are either lost or never internalized. As a result, these youngsters feel incomplete, eternally seeking symbiotic relationships. The drastic impact sexual abuse has upon the child's object relations is clearly reflected in the drawings that follow.

CASE STUDY ANALYSIS OF DRAWINGS

Lois

This 7-year-old child-victim of incest, who was abused by her 14-year-old
live-in cousin, gave indication of her frail ego state in previous drawings
(Plates 25-27, pp. 62–63). Her House Drawing and KFD depict her struggle
with issues of trust, one of the most common sequelae experienced by rape
and incest victims (Brothers, 1982). In Plate 70 we see a tall house with
windows almost exclusively limited to the upper level. In addition to the fact
that this treatment flags a suspicion of sexual abuse (Blain et al., 1981), it
suggests Lois's withdrawal from social contact (Jolles, 1971). Doors afford a
mode of egress and ingress and are equated with accessibility (Buck, 1981).
Lois's very small door is another sign of her lack of trust and reluctance to
allow others access to her. It is not surprising that Lois's drawing projects her
hesitancy to believe in others. No only did a close family member betray her
through his sexual aggression, but also her parents abandoned her through
their inability to protect her against the desecration.

When we look at the Kinetic Family Drawing (Plate 71), a clearer picture of
how Lois perceives her nuclear family is portrayed. Lois's view of her parents'

PLATE 70.

PLATE 71.

self-absorption is reflected in the way they are cut off from each other as well as from both children. Each adult is placed in such a manner that neither is accessible to the children. It is as if they can not even see the youngsters, let alone each other. Clearly, a fertile field for communication does not exist. A powerful sense of isolation abounds. The table appears more like a wall than as an object offering nurturance. In fact, no indication of any food is present. One might wonder if this family is truly sitting down for a meal even though Lois has written "we're eating." The words are there. But that is where it ends. This most likely mirrors how Lois experiences her family. She is told she is loved; yet her tiny figure—the smallest on the page, despite the fact that her sister is only 3—is left to fend for herself.

Tara

This 7-year-old girl was sexually abused by her father and presented earlier with reference to her ego dysfunctions (Plates 34 to 36, p. 70). Here, in her KFD (Plate 72), Tara has drawn her family seated in church on the occasion of her first communion. (Note the words on the upper righthand side of the drawing.) Each family member is individually encapsulated, very similar to the manner in which family members in Plate 71 were compartmentalized by chairs and a table. In the authors' study on the quantitative analysis of drawings of sexually abused youngsters, this specific feature of compartmentalization, or encapsulation, had the most significant correlation to sexual abuse. Tara's KFD also contains other elements associated with sexual abuse, including a multitude of circles (Sidun & Rosenthal, 1987) and a colored-in face (Cohen & Phelps, 1985).

In a qualitative examination of encapsulation, the chairs separate each family member from the other. Tara is further segregated from her mother, stepfather, and brothers by her veil, her posture, and her relative distance from the family. This drawing also graphically portrays the family's alienation from the community at large. This is represented by the priest, the figure on the extreme right, standing outside the church, while Tara and her family remain within its walls.

PLATE 72.

Tara is confused about where she fits in the world. She has placed herself between her family and the priest, but her body posture is ambivalent. Tara's head, torso, and feet face front, while her arms are in profile. Her position portrays her desire to escape from her situation (Jolles, 1971). But perhaps these thoughts, albeit unconscious, are too threatening to Tara for she looks away from the priest. Her face, hair, and hands are darkly shaded, representing her anxiety in facing and reaching out to the priest. The shading of the face actually looks like a mask covering her identity, which, in a way, keeps her from being known.

It's no accident that Tara chose her first communion as the subject matter of this drawing. This event includes the first confession of sins and its representation suggests that Tara has taken on the blame and guilt of the incest and feels sinful. In addition, this religious ceremony is also the first time that a child accepts God. Might this be her defense (reaction formation) against her feelings of badness and evil? These wicked feelings, along with her sense of being different from others, keep her from being able to experience herself as a part of her family. They further hinder her from "breaking through the wall" into society and feeling accepted by others.

Elmer

Elmer's need to structure what he experiences as a threatening world was described in Chapter 3 on ego dysfunctions and seen in Plates 23 and 24 (pp. 60–61). His paternal uncle's fondling of him has left its mark on this 7-year-old. The child's way of relating, a pivotal issue for the developing latency-age child, is problematic. Like Tara, he questions how he and others interface. This can be seen in his House Drawing (Plate 73). The house, as discussed, is an inner

PLATE 73.

ME   SISTER   mommy

PLATE 74.

self-portrait and relates to how a youngster feels about himself and his family. In this drawing, we see a female figure, relatively large in relation to the house, standing beside it. This seems to mirror Elmer's sense that others are unable to enter into his world; his family is a closed system with somewhat impermeable boundaries. The person is too big to get into the house. She literally remains an outsider.

Elmer was asked to draw a picture of a house. Yet, when we look at Plate 73, the house is lost and dwarfed amidst a multiplicity of details. This may well project Elmer's sense of losing himself when involved in a relationship. He is unable to maintain a picture of who he is and becomes absorbed into the environment. The world as Elmer sketched it is filled with hostility. The erect blades of grass are sharp and piercing and, in fact, penetrate the figure between the legs. Three clouds loom above, representing his anxiety about this ominous world.

Two birds fly above it all, portraying Elmer's wish to physically flee from his pressured predicament (Hammer, 1980). His KFD (Plate 74) further alludes to this need. Both Elmer and his sister have bicycles ready to take them away. His bike, on the extreme lefthand side of the drawing, and his sister's, in the center of the drawing, both serve as a barrier between the children and others. This may be a maneuver on his part to create protective boundaries for himself and his sister.

The short arms on all the figures alerts us to Elmer's ineptitude in reaching out to others and to his tendency to withdraw and stay separate (Koppitz, 1968). This is further reflected in the glovelike treatment of the branches in the tree in Plate 73. The stubby branches look like a hand with shortened fingers and suggest, once again, that Elmer's inability to reach out into the environment tends to leave him isolated.

Even though the abuse foisted upon Elmer was not within the nuclear family, his KFD reveals a factor that likely contributed to its inception. Although his mother is supportive and involved with him, this drawing shows us that he experiences her as ineffective in her parenting role. He has sketched her as being considerably smaller than both he and his 3-year-old sister and also has positioned her furthest away from him.

Nancy

Nancy draws a house with most of the expected details much like her Person Drawings (Plates 19 and 20, pp. 56–57), where the figures appeared masked, thereby providing the viewer with the sense that she puts on the proper face. However, her abusive past slants the presentation. The window in the house (Plate 75) in the upper lefthand corner is markedly different from the rest of the

PLATE 75.

windows. This dissimilarity (Cohen & Phelps, 1985) and the presence of wedge shapes (Sidun & Rosenthal, 1987) attest to a history of sexual abuse.

The house created by this 8-year-old youngster has no depth and looks almost like a façade with nothing behind it. This mirrors the barren quality Nancy experiences within her family. Sexually abused by her stepfather for four years and disbelieved and unprotected by her mother, Nancy felt abandoned and forsaken. The House Drawing reflects these feelings. The house appears empty and unlived in. There is no chimney, no smoke, no hint of family warmth. In fact, there is no sense of anything substantive.

Nancy's real self remains inaccessible and unavailable to others. The door is above the baseline of the house and yet there are no steps up to it. There is no way for one to enter (Jolles, 1971). However, the desire for genuine intimacy and involvement is nonetheless present as seen through the position of the house. The house reaches towards the trees. When trees are included in a House Drawing, they often symbolize a significant person in the artist's life (Buck, 1981). While the house gravitates towards the tree, the tree clearly faces away from the house. It leans towards the right and is slightly flattened on the left side. It is as if Nancy presses for contact with her mother, but her mother moves away, remaining unattuned to Nancy's needs much as she did when Nancy disclosed the incest to her.

Ralph

Ralph's Kinetic Family Drawing (Plate 76) tells us a great deal about his perception of his family life. In the PDI Ralph stated that the family was sitting down to a meal. However, the table, the large structure in the center of the drawing, is devoid of food. Much like Lois, presented earlier, this suggests that while he longs for nurturance, it is not forthcoming. This is also reflected by the omission of a chimney and smoke in the House Drawing (Plate 77) (Mursell, 1969). Additionally in the KFD, looming larger than life, is a huge penislike formation that separates Ralph from his twin brother and pet dog. It is as if this reminder of the sexual abuse both boys suffered from their father has created a rift between them. Ralph is even cut off from the warmth of his dog and left alone with his mother.

Ralph's unconscious attempt to regulate and control his contact with others is emphasized by the location of the windows, well above ground level, in the House Drawing (Plate 77). Their placement limits others from seeing in, and the bubblelike panes additionally obfuscate any images. Clearly, secrets are able to be kept. Likewise, this is seen in the skinlike covering of the branches of the tree (Plate 78), which serves to encase the truth (Koch, 1952). Forced to hold back secrets, Ralph must, of necessity, limit his interaction with others. This boundary provides another function. It shields Ralph from others and keeps them away. Let us remember that this youngster has been brutally betrayed and hurt by those closest to him. He has lost his trust in others and needs to protect himself.

The paper-based house (Plate 77) (Jolles, 1971) coupled with the comparative size of Ralph and his mother (Plate 76) (Burns & Kaufman, 1972) imply that Ralph feels he has no one to rely on. His father is literally out of the picture; his

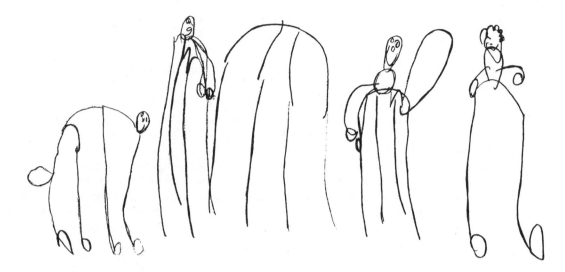

PLATE 76.

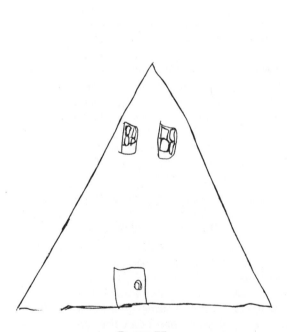

PLATE 77.

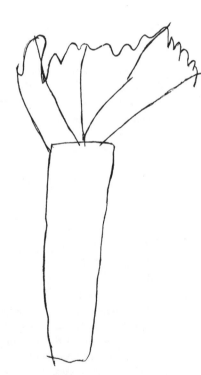

PLATE 78.

mother is not experienced as powerful enough to protect him. Ralph is, thereby, left feeling very insecure. We can conclude from the placement of the figures that he feels he has been relegated to fill his father's shoes. Unfortunately, he has no feet and attempts to compensate for his felt inadequacies with a large batlike arm.

Carole

Hammer (1980) believes that a child's drawing of a person represents either the self, the idealized self, or a parent. The drawing of a person of the opposite sex frequently taps the child's perception of the parent of the opposite sex. For example, 6-year-old Carole has drawn a male in response to the request to "draw a person of the opposite sex." It may, therefore, be assumed that his figure, at least in part, projects the thoughts, feelings, and ideas she associates with her father.

The manner in which Carole depicts this male figure (Plate 79) may signify her perception of her father as an aggressive, dangerous man. This information can be culled by observing the unusually wide stance the figure has assumed in the center of the drawing. This posture and placement conveys overt aggression (Machover, 1980), much like that experienced by Carole at the hands of her father. An additional indication of this is seen through the sharply pointed nose (Ogdon, 1977). Further evidence of Carole's view of him as a hostile force can be seen in the pointed and spiked fingers (Koppitz, 1968) on the figure's left hand (to the viewer, this is the hand on the right side). Koppitz notes that this approach is most frequently drawn by aggressive children. Interestingly, Hammer believes "the kind of perception of mother- or father-figure the child reveals in his drawing is frequently a prophesying element predicting the traits . . . the child incorporates . . . and one is tempted to say . . . [it is a predicator of] . . . the future self" (Hammer, 1980, pp. 198, 200).

To remind the reader, Carole's Person Drawing (Plate 8, p. 47) suggested that she was eager to please others, while at the same time, she was virtually numb to her own feelings. The Person of the Opposite Sex Drawing (Plate 79) implies that, without intervention, Carole will likely grow into a belligerent adult, identifying with the behavior of her aggressive father.

PLATE 79.

Alice

Alice, who is 6, has already been presented (Plates 17, 18, & 49, pp. 54–55, 84) as having a paucity of good enough adults in her life with whom to identify. This has caused her to have problems in the development of a consistent and socially appropriate value system. It was also noted that she tended to utilize regressive defenses, such as denial, as a way of coping. Presently, Alice remains in foster care due to sexual victimization by her stepfather and the lack of attention paid to the abuse by her mother.

The effect of Alice's life experiences on her ability to relate to others is seen in both her House Drawing (Plate 80) and her KFD (Plate 81). How very poignant that this young child has already blocked out her availability to others. Her unusual drawing of a doorless house leaves no question that one cannot enter from the outside. It conveys her "pathoformic difficulty in becoming accessible to others" (Jolles, 1971, p. 47). The shaded doorknob, high up on the house's left side (viewers right side), portrays Alice's heightened concern about the function of a door. This structure enables one to have direct contact with the environment (Hammer, 1980). However, this doorknob serves to open nothing, for there is no door; there is no possibility of any connection to others. The windows, well above eye level, further communicate this same message "stay out," "there's nothing I'll allow you to see." In the KFD (Plate 81), the small size of the building additionally indicates her tendency to withdraw. Its high placement on the paper corroborates her fear of others and reflects her attempt to avoid them. Moreover, the house's size and placement suggest that it is distant from the viewer. This indicates Alice's sense that her home situation is too difficult for her to handle (Ogdon, 1977).

PLATE 81.

PLATE 80.

In further reviewing Alice's Kinetic Family Drawing, it is apparent that the style in which she presents her family and the bizarre quality of the house itself are both atypical. In addition, she identifies this drawing as a "jungle house," which likely represents her perception that the people in her home are out of control. To compensate, she attempts to limit and structure the environment by keeping them within the house and, further, by encapsulating each person individually.

Another important point highlighted in this KFD is that Alice does not differentiate between the various family members. Each person is shown in the same way—through a window in the house. All members are basically of equal size and each is drawn with a smiling face. Although in the PDI Alice explained who the faces represented, in reality, the members are not distinguishable from each other. Despite that fact that each person is isolated from the others, the similar presentation graphically portrays that differences between them are not tolerated. This manner of representing her family also connotes that roles are in no way delineated. Moreover, each person seems to have equal power, although no one has a body to empower her or himself.

Danielle

Danielle's parents divorced when she was 3 years old. Her father had several extramarital affairs prior to the divorce and before selecting 5-year-old Danielle as a sexual partner. Due to ongoing and intense hostility between the parents, Danielle developed a pattern of being both parentified and triangulated. She was frequently privy to information about one parent about which the other knew nothing. Her mother confided nasty tidbits to her about her father, while he often put the child in situations unbeknownst to her mother.

For example, Danielle would be in the company of her father's girlfriends and told not to tell her mother. This provided a fertile environment for Danielle to keep secrets. This is one of the important components necessary for an incestuous relationship to be continued. As such, once the incest began, Danielle was unfortunately primed to remain silent. But after a few months of vaginal manipulation by her father, she told her mother about the abuse. Her case went to court. However, like those of other children in her situation, Danielle's testimony was not believed, and the charges were dismissed. This dismissal happened despite a corroborating statement by her 7-year-old brother who had witnessed the acts.

Danielle's drawings bear testimony to her sexual molestation. Identified indicators of sexual abuse are scattered throughout them. Her Human Figure Drawing (Plate 82) has a number of extraneous circles on the face and chest area, and a wedge-shaped nose, skirt, and the foot on the left side. As noted previously, these items have been correlated with child sexual abuse. In addition, Danielle identifies two of the six circles on the chest as breasts. The presence of genitalia in a drawing is a strong indicator suggesting sexual violation (Hibbard et al., 1987; Kelley, 1985).

The left foot (which appears to the right for the viewer) on the male figure (Plate 83) is triangular. In addition this figure has extra circles on the face, chest, right hand (left side of the page), and between the legs. One wonders whether the circle between the legs is a suggested penis. The House Drawing

PLATE 82.

PLATE 83.

PLATE 84.

PLATE 85.

(Plate 84) has one window treated differently than the others. This, too, has been found to be a probable signal of sexual abuse (Cohen & Phelps, 1985).

In viewing Danielle's artwork more interpretatively, her projective drawings yield cue to her interpersonal difficulties. The multiplicity of chimneys in the House Drawing (Plate 84) catches one's attention. This treatment is associated with an overconcern about the phallus and close relationships. This link between the sexual symbol and interpersonal relationships might suggest a correlation between her victimization and her problems relating to others.

The chimneys, the structures through which warmth for the family is facilitated, expresses Danielle's anxiety about familial tenderness and devotedness. The two chimneys, flanking the sides of the house, likely represent her parents' separate households. The structure in the middle, a less definitive form, seems to suggest the remnant of a family once united. Smoke emanates only from the peripheral chimneys. The single thin lines of smoke, however, connote her experienced lack of family affection (Jolles, 1971).

These same problems are portrayed through treatment in her Tree Drawing (Plate 85). The overly large branch structure, which extends beyond the paper's upper edge, graphically speaks of Danielle's intense concern with having her needs adequately met by others (Jolles, 1971). This anxiety is echoed in her female Person Drawing (Plate 82) by the long arms that are suggestive of her need for her mother's protection (Machover, 1980). All children require their parent's care. A child presumes, on the basis of his or her experience, that it will be present. This need, therefore, does not have to be emphasized, as it is here. Its presence thus implies that Danielle, for the most part, feels abandoned.

Danielle is clearly a bright girl. This can be gleaned from the sophisticated details she includes in her renderings. Nonetheless, her tragic life bears emotional scars that, despite her attempts, her intellect cannot overcome. The placement of the tree, high on the page, intimates Danielle's withdrawal from others. Her propensity to isolate herself is also reflected in her elevated door (Plate 84). Placed well above the base of the house, and smaller even than the windows, neither its size nor location allows entry. This reflects Danielle's difficulty in trusting others. She cannot take the chance to permit others access to her. Further confirmation of her tendency to keep the environment at bay is indicated by the large female drawing (Plate 82). It is as if the figure fills up the entire space and there is no room for anyone else in her world. This is clearly defensive, as these drawings communicate Danielle's felt lack of parental care.

Sidney

Sidney was the unfortunate victim of his 18-year-old brother's sexual perversions. For over six months the brothers engaged in mutual masturbation. In addition, Sidney was forced to undress under the watchful and leering eye of his sibling. During this period, their father was out of work and financial difficulties preoccupied the parents' thoughts and actions. For 6-year-old Sidney, the abuse became unbearable and he finally told his mother. She, in turn, confronted her older son who then confessed. The abuse was put to rest, but its mark remained etched in Sidney's psyche. Although no information was

PLATE 86.

PLATE 87.

PLATE 88.

available to the testers, one wonders what instigated the abuse and if, in fact, the perpetrating sibling was not himself a victim at some earlier time, who was now defending against his own helplessness by identifying with the aggressor.

Sidney's Kinetic Family Drawing (Plate 86) is a graphic statement that expresses his perception of his role within the family system. Clearly the largest and most powerful figure, he portrays himself as riding a bicycle. Yet his dominant and parentified position does not sit well with him; he is precariously balanced above the seat. Sidney tries to create distance between himself and his mother (figure to his left); yet, the only erasure on the page occurs on his left arm. In reworking this appendage, Sidney enlarged it, thus depicting both his determination and conflict about holding her off. Perhaps it is not just her but his entire family from which he is trying to separate, for his father and brother are the figures to the mother's left. Be that as it may, his position puts great strain on him. In fact, his seated pose, and his distortion in the relative sizes of the family members, connote his conflict over his action (Koppitz, 1968; Machover, 1980). His effort to create boundaries between himself and his family members throws him off balance and leaves him in danger of tumbling. But if he falls, he will fall into the figures he added to the lefthand side of the page. These extra people represent Sidney's attempt to provide substitutes to sit in for the family he experiences as insufficiently nuturing.

Given this family picture, it is no surprise to the observer that Sidney has significant problems in his interpersonal relations. In his drawings of the boy (Plate 87) and the girl (Plate 88), he drew the legs first, added the body and arms and, last, the head. This sequence is generally used by youngsters who have difficulty relating to others (Koppitz, 1968). These drawings also say that Sidney is an angry child. The presence of the teeth on both figures reveals his propensity for oral aggression, namely, the biting use of words. In addition, the teeth depict his inclination for sadistic actions. Within this context, there is concern that Sidney may come to identify with his brother and become a future abuser.

The short arms present on both figures reflect Sidney's difficulty in reaching out to others. It is as if he is trying to inhibit his aggressive and sexual impulses (Koppitz, 1968). Another indicator of this tendency to inhibit his inclinations is seen in the tiny eyes. This treatment is associated with individuals who show strong visual curiosity but, in fact, have guilt linked to this function. It may be in the nature of a voyeuristic conflict. These tiny eyes represent Sidney's desire to be connected with others, but in a limited and controlled manner.

In ascertaining the quality of contact that Sidney has had with others, the direction of the arms is significant. The arms on all the figures Sidney has drawn extend directly out from the bodies. However, their somewhat mechanical position cannot be considered an actual extension into the world and, instead, convey Sidney's shallow and unemotional contact with people (Machover, 1980). Moreover, their winglike presentation is reflective of Sidney's tendency to withdraw (Gurvitz, 1951). Sidney's superficial involvement with others may be related to his lack of trust. The reinforced ears, whose very presence is unusual, is most often drawn by paranoid individuals who are guarded, suspicious, and distrustful (Machover, 1980).

Robert

Eleven-year-old Robert was sexually abused by his maternal grandfather for over one year. His sister and cousin Jane were, likewise, involved in molestations perpetrated by this man, who had also violated his own daughter when she was a child. Although the grandfather confessed to molesting Robert, the specifics of the abuse are not known. However, based on play therapy sessions, it was suspected that there had been anal penetration.

Robert's House Drawing (Plate 89), created without a baseline, mirrors the lack of a solid familial foundation. Moreover, the structure is so open-ended

PLATE 89.

PLATE 90.

PLATE 91.

PLATE 92.

that boundaries between it and the environment are virtually nonexistent. The door treatment leaves one confused as to whether the door is open or closed. This may represent Robert's ambivalence towards contact with others. If the door is open, then Robert is vulnerable to whatever comes along. If it is closed—since there is no doorknob with which to open it—Robert remains shut off from the outside world.

This evasiveness is also reflected in the profile positions of both the male and female persons (Plates 90 and 91 respectively). This view represents his hesitancy to face and communicate with others (Buck, 1973). It also reveals serious withdrawal tendencies (Urban, 1963). The face is the most expressive part of a person and the pivotal point of contact. A side view therefore constricts and skews the way one is seen in the world. One cannot get the full picture of another from such a limited perspective. This reluctance to become involved with others is also seen by the arms which press closely and rigidly against the body. The Tree Drawing (Plate 92), whose branch structure does not extend into the outer world, gives further evidence of Robert's evasive character structure.

Since fingers "are the real contact points" (Machover, 1980, p. 63) with the environment, and enter children's drawings even before the hands, their omission (Plates 90 & 91) is very telling. It also reveals Robert's severe problem relating to others. Fingers are not only vehicles for communication. Even more, they carry the potential for hostile acts. The absence of this important body part denotes Robert's effort to contain his aggressive impulses. His propensity to act out shows up in the way he handled the paper for the House Drawing. It was handed to him vertically, but he turned it horizontally. This symbolizes an oppositional quality (Hammer, 1980). The profile view of the two figures (Plates 90 & 91) also confirms this proclivity (Urban, 1963).

Robert's specific relationship to his family is revealed through his KFD (Plate 93). He places himself closest to his mother, the largest figure, by far, on the page. This symbolizes the important position she holds for him. However, she is depicted facing away from him, which portrays his impression that she is not forthright and available. Likewise, his father—who is farthermost from him on the page and faces away from everyone else in the family—is inaccessible.

PLATE 93.

Within the context of this family, Robert seems diminutive and poorly developed. This reveals his sense of relative insignificance. His mother looms over him, seemingly wedging herself between Robert and the rest of the family but offering nothing for her immense presence.

Kenny

Kenny's parents separated when he was 3 years old. Although Kenny lived with his mother, he and his father had regular contact on a weekly basis. These visits provided the highlight of his week. About a year after the divorce, his mother began to notice that Kenny was exhibiting sexually suggestive behaviors. She initially thought it was part of normal development but the posturing became increasingly alarming. She started to question Kenny about his actions. At first he ignored her inquiries but eventually disclosed that his father and his father's girlfriend both engaged in sexual exposure and masturbation with him. When his mother filed charges the authorities viewed her allegations with suspicion because the divorce had been acrimonious.

Frustrated and bordering on panic because visitation with the father was continuing, the mother pressured Kenny to repeat his story time and again to her, as well as to others. Although it was unintentional, this constant badgering exacerbated Kenny's symptoms, leading the authorities to suggest that he be evaluated for treatment. He was an extremely anxious and regressed child, and at the point of clinical assessment, the basis for his presenting problems was clouded. The question of whether there had been sexual abuse or whether the mother was histrionic and overreacting was left unanswered. As of this writing, Kenny has completed two years of treatment at a local child guidance center that specializes in sexual abuse. It is their clinical conclusion that he was sexually abused by his father and his father's girlfriend.

Kenny's three drawings, of a Person (Plate 94), of a Person of the Opposite Sex (Plate 95) and a House Drawing (Plate 96), were gathered at the point of intake when he was 5 years old. Despite the drawing's suggestion of neurological impairment, psychological testing revealed that his problems were emotionally based. Moreover, even though the organization of the details give the figures a bizarre appearance (Plates 94 and 95), the presence of the two-dimensional eyes, including pupils and eyelids, and two-dimensional bodies, feet, and hands suggest that he was a bright boy in psychological distress. This manifested in such a high level of anxiety that it seriously interfered with his school performance and peer relationships.

It is not only the acts of sexual violation that have impeded Kenny's functioning, but also the reverberations of his connection to his mother. As has been noted earlier in this text, drawings of figures of the opposite sex often reveal the child's attitudes about that parent. The female figure (Plate 95) is a poignant portrayal of Kenny's feelings for his mother. Looming ominously and taking up most of the page, she initially appears powerful. In fact, he places himself, metaphorically through his name, under her skirt. Like a young child, he seeks her protective shelter.

Yet he has an awareness that she is incapable of providing true safety. The heavily shaded one-dimensional arms are weighed down by huge hands. They

PLATE 94.

PLATE 95.

PLATE 96.

are unable to reach out or lift him. In fact, the large hands are symbolic of a tendency to behave impulsively (Jolles, 1971). Further examination of the drawing reveals that Kenny experiences his mother as a malevolent person. The figure's wide stance is regarded as a suggestion of overt aggression (Machover, 1980). In addition, the large hovering, angry face, to the figure's left, may connote that Kenny splits off his mother's aggression. He displaces this onto the environment and encounters the world as hostile and threatening.

Kenny's sense of how the abuse has affected his mother is expressed through the woman's distorted alignment. It is almost as if the pressure of dealing with Kenny's defilement has left her off center. She cannot think straight and is not well-balanced. Another factor that must be addressed in Kenny's view of a female is the part that the father's girlfriend played in his life. She was a menacing, intrusive, and assaultive presence.

The aggressive sexual invasion and his concomitant disturbed relationship with his mother have distorted Kenny's ability to adequately move within the world. This is reflected in his Person Drawing of a male (Plate 94). The arms and legs are barely distinguishable amongst the profusion of line and movement. There is a sense of chaos and lack of direction in his interaction with the environment. The heavily shaded arms and feet suggest the anxiety Kenny experiences when he makes contact with others.

Perhaps that is why his house (Plate 96) is so enclosed and allows no entrance. There are no windows and the large, heaving shaded door lacks a doorknob. Likewise, the male figure (Plate 94) is placed well above the mid-point of the page, symbolizing Kenny's desire to remain aloof (Jolles, 1971). Returning to the house, note that although it appears fiery, there is no warmth—there is no chimney and no smoke (Hammer, 1980). This is sadly predictable; all the significant adults in Kenny's life, up to the time of these drawings, were experienced as intrusive and aggressive towards him. His home life resulted in his development as an anxious and uncontrollable child. The short, discontinuous strokes, which define the house, reflect this impulsive and excitable tendency (Hammer, 1980).

CONCLUSION

Latency is the time when consolidation of earlier developmental phases take place. Sexually assaulted children, like other youngsters, now gingerly stepping onto the community path, carry in their backpacks the book of family lessons. It is not something they must learn, for it is etched into their basic characters. They cannot relate to another without the preponderant influence of their earlier years. The meaning these youngsters attribute to the abuse, to the abuser, and to the actions and attitudes of other family members is extraordinarily significant.

It is the children's internal experience of these combined forces that affects their psychological makeup and characterizes how they will interpret the behavior and feelings of others in the future. They will relate to individuals such as teachers with love, rejection, hate, or admiration not because of who the teachers are or what they do, but because of how these people are associated to these youngsters' earlier experiences with others. Abused children are scarred by dysfunctional models of relating and caring, which have been saturated with neglect, force, molestation, and a lack of validation. Ruthless sexual exploitation shatters these youngsters' sense of participatory equality. Their self-images become shadowed and blackened by the inequality of their role in the relationship and are forever darkened by their view of their inability to relate.

CHAPTER 6

ADULT SURVIVORS:
THE LONG-TERM EFFECTS
OF CHILDHOOD SEXUAL ABUSE

The material discussed thus far has elucidated the derailment of the latency-age child's developmental goals due to the impact of sexual abuse. The difficulties generated by the molestations most often continue to surface in future developmental stages, impeding both the individual's age-appropriate functioning and his or her ability to progress through life. The sexual abuse of the child leaves its indelible mark on the adult into which he or she develops. When children are sexually molested by the trusted adults upon whom they depend, their basic concepts of self and the world are severely shaken. The youngster's character structure, self-image, self-esteem, trust in self and others take on different and new forms.

In a sense, the child who existed prior to the trauma has been murdered. The new child who emerges will most likely be jaded and damaged. The grown-up child as an adult, then, bears only a shadow of resemblance to the mature person he or she might otherwise have become. The exploitation has marred future possibilities for it has become the central organizer of experiences.

Unless interventions are made, the pattern of childhood sexual abuse tends to play itself out time and again throughout the life cycle (Briere & Runtz, 1987). Sometimes, the adult becomes a victim of multiple sexual abusers; other times, abusive mates are chosen. In still other situations, individual survivors may view their world through the distorted and stained visions of their youthful experiences. Kindness is viewed with suspicion; closeness is felt as invasion; benevolent acts are seen as malevolent; malevolent actions are expected. In still other instances, these individuals tragically endure all the scenarios. They become perpetual victims, victimize themselves, or may identify with the aggressor and become perpetrators. Adults are profoundly affected by traumas of childhood: ego, superego, and object relations are scarred. The depth of the scar will vary, but in some shape or form it will most probably remain present. "The effects are not simply psychological in nature; they affect ... [the person's] ... life course, ... life style ... and attitudes" (Finkelhor, Hotaling, Lewis, & Smith, 1989, p. 396).

EGO DYSFUNCTIONS

The problems of the ego that were caused by sexual abuse in childhood often continue to plague the adult. Coping mechanisms that the youngster originally developed as survival tactics become maladaptive later in life. Dissociation is a common strategy deployed by the child-victim (Briere & Runtz, 1987). While dissociative defenses, such as becoming part of the wall, floating on the ceiling, or pretending to be elsewhere, may be useful tools used by the child to maintain a sense of personal control and power during the abuse, for the adult these become unwelcome obstructions, often creating a conscious experience of confusion (Gelinas, 1983).

Depersonalization, another way the child-victim cuts off from an intolerable situation, is a highly dysfunctional adult state. Multiple Personality Disorders, representing the most extreme form of dissociation, can develop in response to extreme, violent, and ongoing sexual abuse perpetrated by family members (Coons, 1986). Research indicates that at least 80% of Multiple Personality Disorders are precipitated by childhood sexual abuse (Coons, 1986; Ross, Norton, & Wozney, 1989).

The regulation of affects appears to be another area that bears the legacy of the childhood violation. The distancing described above has the potential to become part of the victim's own emotional state, which leads to a circumstance of internal deadness eventuating in alexithymia. The emotions evoked during the trauma were so excruciating that the child repressed and disowned them, creating a permanent change in his affective life (Krystal, 1988). Depression, another chronic sequela and the most common response to childhood incest, afflicts many adult survivors. This is particularly true for those survivors who have been unable to express the rage and fury they have felt about the violations.

Others identify with their perpetrators and become the victimizers in relationships (Peters, 1978). Handling both their own anger and anger directed at them often becomes a lifelong struggle for adult survivors. The affective life of adult victims is often so painful that they need to numb themselves. Some turn to drugs and alcohol as a method of self-medication aimed at self-soothing. In fact, research has shown that this population has a higher rate of substance abuse than the population of nonvictims (Finkelhor et al., 1989).

The intensity of survivors' lifelong stress not only takes its psychological toll, but often leads to physical problems. As a result, many survivors exhibit symptoms of physical illness (Shapiro, 1987). Waigandt, Wallace, Phelps and Miller (1990), who conducted a study investigating the long-term physical health implications of sexual abuse, found statistically significant evidence that assault victims suffered from enduring physical difficulties.

Psychosomatic symptoms appear to be particularly prevalent among incest victims (Forward & Buck, 1978; Kaufman et al., 1954). These include migraines, gastrointestinal disturbances, dizziness, skin disorders, female reproductive ailments, and other aches and pains. It is as if sexual abuse victims are more psychologically prepared to deal with physical pain and discomfort than to face the emotional tension, anxieties, and conflicts associated with the abuse. They express their distress through their bodies.

ABERRATIONS IN THE SUPEREGO

Just as ego dysfunctions emanating from childhood affect the adult, likewise, superego aberrations follow the child into adulthood. Self-mutilation is a frequent characteristic present in adult survivors. This behavior can be interpreted as a disturbance in the superego from the perspective that the survivor is engaged in a form of self-punishment. It is common for victims to blame themselves for the abuse they have suffered and then feel guilty. Guilt plays "an essential role in . . . the victims' . . . everyday functioning, self-identity, and estimation of what they are legitimately entitled to. . . . They . . . express guilt about the occurrence . . . and usually blame themselves" (Gelinas, 1983, p. 322).

In time, this feeling may culminate with acts of self-injury (Shapiro, 1987). Some survivors repeatedly engage in "delicate cutting," during which they gently scratch their skin with a razor or other sharp object. These adults are not intending to commit suicide, but rather are expressing their emotional pain. However, suicidal ideation and attempts are also the unfortunate and common sequelae to child sexual abuse (Briere & Runtz, 1987). Maisch (1972) notes that one-third of the sexually abused daughters in his study tried to kill themselves.

Low self-esteem, another legacy that the adult survivor inherits from childhood, can be defined as the absence of a basic respect and liking for oneself. It follows that the self-esteem of a victim of sexual trauma will be seriously affected (Steele & Alexander in Mrazek & Kempe, 1981). Studies investigating the long-term effects of sexual abuse indicate that it is common for adult survivors to report negative feelings about themselves that they link to the earlier molestation (Herman, Russell, & Trocki, 1986). Frequently, they act out these feelings, and perpetuate them, through promiscuity and prostitution (Gelinas, 1983).

DISTURBANCES IN OBJECT RELATIONS

Relational disturbances are also frequent in sexual abuse victims. Peer interactions are thwarted partly because, as children, there was preoccupation with sexual impulses. These children frequently have very few friends. Although they may desire friendship, they have learned to distrust intimacy. This tends to isolate these youngsters, who then grow up feeling different from peers. The grown-up victim continues to feel isolated and lonely.

In incestuous families, the child-victims are often parentified, becoming the caretakers. As adults, these survivors continue their earlier role. They often marry infantile mates who act out. As a result, the victim once more is trapped into providing care for another. Unfortunately, the victim often unconsciously seeks a dysfunctional partner in order to reenact earlier family problems.

Many authors (Everstine & Everstine, 1989; Katan, 1973; Kaufman et al., 1954) note that victims of sexual abuse develop a disturbance in their sexual identity. The victimization skews their sense of sexuality, creating a distorted understanding about sex roles. Sometimes a female child may identify with the abuser and focus on the acquisition of a penis. As an adult, she may then prefer a male identity, which she sees as undamaged and powerful. In other instances, when the attacker of a male is a male, the victim's sense of himself may be threatened. Experiencing himself as powerless and weak, as well as the receiver of the penis, he may identify more with the female role.

Some studies have linked male and female homosexuality with child sexual abuse. But regardless of whether an adult survivor favors a homosexual or heterosexual relationship, there tends to be a prevalence of sexual difficulties. For incest victims especially, there is a propensity of orgasmic dysfunctions as well as difficulty with sexual contact (Gelinas, 1983). For instance, if penile penetration was part of the molestation, the victim may have an aversion to engage in sexual activity that involves a penis.

Most research agrees that child sexual abuse has long-term effects on the victim (Briere & Runtz, 1987; Herman et al., 1986; Kaufman et al., 1954; Krystal, 1988). Sometimes these marks are not visible for years and emerge in adulthood at milestones such as marriage, the birth of a child, or when the victim's child becomes the age at which the victim was victimized.

Life events subsequent to the abuse affect the severity of the victim's symptoms and personality disturbances. As mentioned earlier, there is a cadre of factors that influence the impact of the trauma. When the adult survivor has had positive people in his or her life, including therapists, friends, mates, and family members, this directly mitigates against long-term negative consequences.

CASE STUDY ANALYSIS OF DRAWINGS

In the following pages, the projective drawings of a diverse group of women survivors of sexual molestation will be presented. These individuals were subjected to a variety of sexual abuses, occurring at different ages for varying lengths of time. Some of the molestations were perpetrated by family members; others were committed by nonfamily members. The victims come from a range of socioeconomic backgrounds, having both intact and broken families. Some have been multiply traumatized. Some of the survivors have had early interventions; other have had none. As we did with the childrens' drawings, the images created by these adult survivors of childhood sexual abuse will be examined to see how they project ego, superego, and object relations strengths and dysfunctions.

Teressa

At the time 33-year-old Teressa created the projective drawings, she was separated from her husband. Together they had one natural daughter and one

PLATE 97.

PLATE 98.

PLATE 99.

PLATE 100.

PLATE 101.

PLATE 102.

foster child. The latter was sexually molested by her husband. Her own sexual abuse, multiply foisted by her father, uncle, and a friend, began when she was 5 and continued for 24 years. Starting with nudity, it progressed to lingering and intimate kisses, mutual fondling, masturbation and oral sex, vaginal- and rectal-digital penetration, finally culminating in genital intercourse. Plagued by symptoms resulting from the abuse, Teressa sought out individual and group therapy for "survivors of sexual abuse." She had been involved with these supports for two years.

Examining Teressa's six drawings, the effects of her victimization become visible. Her House Drawing (Plate 97) looks rather pleasant and inviting upon first view, containing all the expected details. This is reminiscent of the children's drawings in which all that is anticipated is dutifully present. Teressa tries to conform to expectations. In fact, there is evidence that she has an extremely rigid and punitive superego. Her Person Drawing (Plate 98) and her Person of the Opposite Sex Drawing (Plate 99) are sketches of a Nun and Jesus Christ, thereby representing her strong identification with very strict moral ethics.

Teressa's need to comply with outside demands is further exemplified in her treatment of the Tree's branch structure (Plate 100). When she produced the six projective drawings, she first drew the House, then started the Tree, stopped to sketch the two Person Drawings and the two KFDs (Plates 101 & 102). She then returned to the drawing of the tree, taking over one and a half hours to complete it. In using this excessive amount of time, she was expressing the strong symbolic value the branch structure holds for her (Buck, 1973). Normally, the entire projective series takes somewhere between five and 40 minutes.

The quantity and quality of Teressa's tree crown, which is rich with subtle ramifications, projects her intense sensitivity and impressionability (Koch, 1952). It is almost as if there are an infinite number of hands reaching out in all directions—would-be feelers trying to get a pulse of the environment. These feelers represent her hypervigilance and excessive need to sense exactly what is happening around her and, in turn, how she should then respond.

Although Teressa tries her best to satisfy her punitive superego, she is unable to measure up. The house, from the outside, looks fine. However, in the PDI, she states that its worst part is the inside, thereby indicating her low self-esteem. In part, these negative feelings are related to her guilt over her own sexual impulses.

In both Person Drawings, the bodies are conspicuously absent, thereby mirroring her denial of her bodily impulses. Further, Teressa chooses a nun to represent her female person (Plate 98) and Jesus Christ (Plate 99) as the male, projecting an ego ideal exemplified by pure and celibate religious figures. However, this may be a reaction formation, for she is not free of conflict regarding her impulses.

Moreover, symbols of the sexual abuse she experienced are strewn throughout the six drawings. Note, in the house, the wedges present in the front windows and door and in the shape of the birds. Wedges are also found in the form of the beard in Plate 99, the "V" configuration of the ribbon holding the cross in Plate 98, and in both KFDs. Circles are also significantly present in the KFDs. Another graphic indicator of sexual abuse, the absence of hands and fingers (Sidun & Rosenthal, 1987), is also reflected in these family drawings.

Teressa's desire for the unbridled release of her impulses is reflected in her Kinetic Family Drawing of her current family (Plate 102). In this rendering, she draws herself and her daughter together on a motorcycle ready to move into action. Her yearning to let go is strong. Yet, the figures wear helmets, which hide the people behind the acts. This concealment is also seen in her House Drawing where all the windows are above ground level, and the front windows are curtained. Although Teressa has a strong desire to know exactly where others are at, as expressed through her tree, she does not reveal herself either to herself or to others.

Unfortunately, this is an expected consequence of sexual abuse. After being molested for 24 years it would be hard for Teressa to trust others and to let them know her. We see in the KFD of her family of origin (Plate 101) that at age 7 she already felt segregated from her mother and brother. Moreover, she felt ambivalent about her connection to her father; although she is closest to him, a barbecue stands between them. Interestingly, it is a hot grill, possibly symbolic of their heated interaction.

Rosalie

The sexual abuse for 54-year-old Rosalie began when she was 4 years old and lasted for seven years. Perpetrated by her stepfather, it involved a full spectrum of sexual abuses ranging from fondling to intercourse. She also experienced a number of disruptions in her early caretaking. She never knew her father, and when she was 9 months old, she was placed in an orphanage where she remained until she was 4. At that time, her mother, who had remarried, reclaimed her. Rosalie then lived with her mother, stepfather, and stepbrothers. When she was 10, one of her stepbrothers was removed from the home. One year later, her mother and stepfather separated. She remained with her mother until her own marriage. Currently divorced, Rosalie has two children, one of whom was also sexually abused as a child, although the identity of the perpetrator is unknown. Rosalie has been in therapy for 20 years trying to recover from her early traumas.

In trying to understand Rosalie through her projective drawings, we are presented with a number of paradoxes. In her House Drawing (Plate 103), a pathway leads to the door. Normally, such a walkway symbolizes a person who invites contact from others (Hammer, 1954). However, this path is littered with rocks, which suggests that approaching Rosalie can be difficult. Then, upon reaching the house, one is greeted by double doors, which generally connote social accessibility (Jolles, 1971). However, this allusion is negated by the double X's almost crossing out the entrance. This seems to reflect Rosalie's desire to have others close to her, while at the same time keeping them at a distance.

This ambivalence is also communicated in the window treatment on the left side of the ground floor. The large window with many panes implies both her caution in letting others get close and her longing to do so (Jolles, 1971). The varied treatment of the other windows expresses this same theme. The use of shades on the upper level keeps others at bay, while the relatively open window on the main floor invites contact. The shrubs outside the front of the house further demonstrate Rosalie's attempt to keep connections relatively remote and formal (Buck, 1981).

The Tree Drawing (Plate 104) presents the viewer with this same symbolic message. While Rosalie works hard at creating a multitude of branches, their organization is ill-defined and muddled. Again, as in the House Drawing, her strong wish to relate is present, but the confused branch treatment shows that her skills in interpersonal relationships are lacking. The roots give the impression of a hand grasping to hold on to something. However, the shading in the branches suggests her extreme anxiety around contact. Rosalie's KFD (Plate 105) is a clear statement of her perception of the source of this problem. She draws her parents having sex, while she and her stepbrothers watch. Her model for closeness is then a primitive and frightening experience.

Interestingly, when Rosalie was asked to draw a person of the opposite sex, she chose to draw her stepfather (Plate 106). Sketched much larger than the woman (Plate 107), who she stated represented herself, the viewer experiences the power and influence this man has had on her life. She remarked in the PDI that his best feature was that he was dead. Yet, here he is almost larger

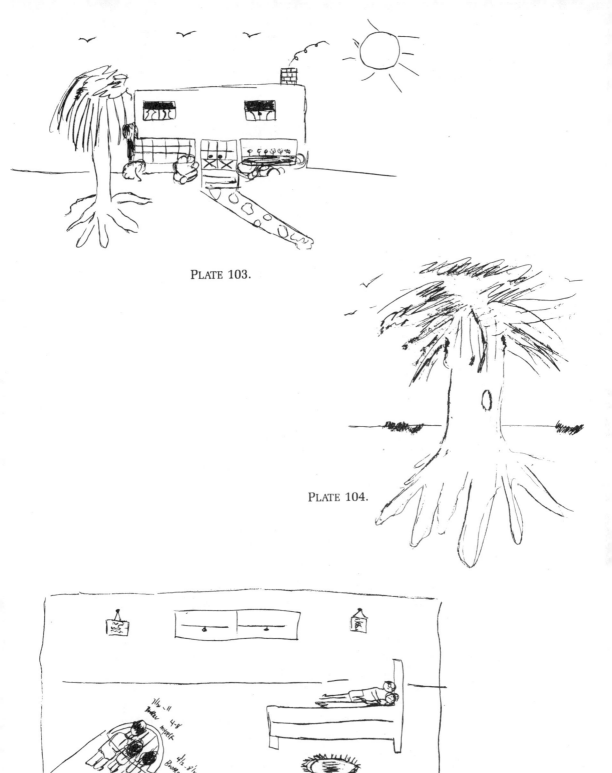

PLATE 103.

PLATE 104.

PLATE 105.

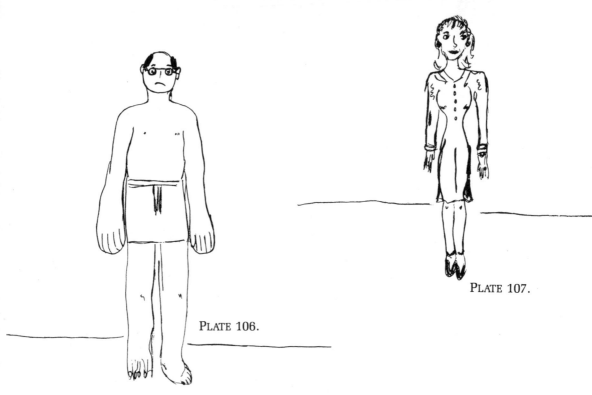

PLATE 107.

PLATE 106.

than life. His large hands project Rosalie's sense of his poor impulse control. But she "mittens" them as a way of limiting their potency. However, this figure has shaped and formed her identity and sense of self as is evident in the Person Drawing (Plate 107). This female is highly sexualized with emphasis on the mouth, eyelashes, hairdo, earrings, hourglass figure, sensuous breasts, and jewelry. In terms of her own self-image and self-worth, sexuality is paramount. Yet, the five buttons in the center of the dress point to her unsatisfied dependency needs, which have left her feeling needy and dependent (Levy, 1950).

In order to make some sense of her early traumas, Rosalie has distorted her life experience, since her perceptions were not validated by the outside world. This has left her with a poor sense of reality. This is reflected by the transparencies present in three of her five drawings. Note in the House Drawing that the house is visible through the shrubs; in the female Person Drawing, the legs show through the lower part of the dress; and in the KFD, the penetration of the penis is visible through the vagina, and the children's bodies are seen through the covers on the bed. The tiptoe stance of the female (Plate 107) is a final confirmation of how poorly Rosalie is footed in reality (Hammer, 1954; Urban, 1963).

Rosalie has attempted to come to terms with her horrendous life by spending 20 years in therapy. Despite this, the mechanisms of avoidance and depersonalization, which were likely developed in childhood and helped her survive, have remained her means of coping as an adult. These defenses are reflected in her drawings. The KFD (Plage 105) depicts the three children with their backs towards the viewer, symbolizing the defense of avoidance (Levick, 1983). The birds in Plates 103 and 104 are another metaphor of Rosalie's wish to flee and avoid her stressful existence (Hammer, 1980). Most dramatically, when asked to draw a KFD of her present family, she left a blank page, avoiding the pain of her current family situation.

Depersonalization, her other major defense, is reflected in the House Drawing (Plate 103) through the broken lines in the wall (Jolles, 1971). The walls of the house represent the ego. When the lines defining the walls are interrupted, the symbolic continuity of the self is broken and there is a sense of being out of touch and distanced from a part of the self. Depersonalization is also seen in the Tree Drawing (Plate 104), where the groundline is above the base of the trunk (Koch, 1952). Again, there is the depiction of remoteness and distance between the tree and the earth. Pictorially, there is a distance from what exists. Reality is, thereby, far removed. The house is also drawn towards the background, symbolically representing Rosalie's wish to stay apart from herself, her affects, and her experiences.

Mary

Forty-five-year-old Mary was sexually abused by her mother during her very early years. Although the abuse only lasted from ages 2 and a half until 4, the effects of the heinous acts have persisted throughout Mary's life. To this date Mary is unable to speak about the details of the molestation without decompensating. The only aspect of the abuse she has been able to verbalize is that it involved cunnilingus. Although the direct abuse stopped when she was a preschooler, she was exposed to her parents' habitual sexual activity for a good part of her latency years. As a teenager, she sought out psychotherapy to help her deal with the many feelings that were beginning to overwhelm her. Sadly, this experience was a repeat of her early relationship with her mother, for the female therapist began to have a sexual relationship with her eventuating in their cohabitation.

Currently, Mary is basically dysfunctional. She is supported by disability and has not worked for many years. She was able to complete college as a science major and taught school for a brief period before her first breakdown. She has superior intelligence and a good sense of humor, which initially enabled her to cope. However, the pathological forms of survival that she developed in response to the abuse also cripple her as an adult. She believes that she is a male and pads her underwear to give the impression of having a penis. She also changed her name to that of a man's. She dresses as a man and is open about being a lesbian. Although her sexual orientation is that of a male, she has not dated for years and has few social contacts. She frequently becomes extremely depressed and has been hospitalized on numerous occasions for psychotic breaks. She has been diagnosed as having a schizoaffective disorder. Mary is currently in therapy and on psychotropic medication.

Mary's drawings reflect her uneven ego development. As mentioned, she is very bright and this is reflected in the language used to describe the drawings. For example, she described her mother as lewd and lascivious in the Kinetic Family Drawing (Plate 108), demonstrating her excellent vocabulary. On the other hand, her reality testing, another essential ego function, is poor. Transparencies are present in all five drawings, representing her dysfunction in this area. The flattened and open tree top (Plate 109) mirrors Mary's attempt to control fantasies but shows her inability to differentiate between the imagined and the real (Hammer, 1980). Additionally, the discontinuity in the branch

Father

Sister Mother

PLATE 108.

PLATE 109.

PLATE 110.

PLATE 112.

PLATE 111.

structure represents disturbances in her thinking (Koch, 1952); and the talonlike roots project her overconcern with her grasp of reality (Hammer, 1980).

The treatment of the house (Plate 110) with two somewhat separate, although connected, sections is curious. The authors believe that this may be a graphic representation of either of two defensive maneuvers, splitting and/or dissociation. One section goes one way, while the other goes in an alternate direction. It is as if Mary has created an alternate space for herself, much like the way the defenses of dissociation and splitting function to create separateness from an overwhelming situation. Mary has been traumatized by the abusive nature of her relationship with her mother. The house (Plate 110), representing home and family life, reflects the effects of this trauma. It is drawn in an unusual triple perspective (note that three sides of the building are seen simultaneously), connoting the crippling effect environmental pressures have had upon her (Buck, 1981).

Notice, also the shrubs that are sketchily placed in front of the house. These portray Mary's struggle to maintain ego boundaries. The shrubs also tell us that Mary tends to structure her contact with others. But this formality can only exist once a person can get close enough to her. This is quite a challenge particularly if one looks at the pathway leading to the house. Just where it begins and goes to are perplexing. In addition, the high placement of the house on the page signals that Mary is fearful of her environment (Buck, 1981).

The feelings evoked in the viewer when looking at the Kinetic Family Drawing (Plate 108) echo these fears. If one imagines oneself as Mary (the figure on the lower right), it is easy to feel terrified. Tiny and helplessly holding up a stop sign, she is almost unnoticeable.

However, while there is the anxiety and trepidation in relation to the family, there is also an attachment. Mary, her mother, and her sister are all shaded, representing not only anxiety, but also commonality. More striking is the similarity between the mother's position in the KFD and the female's posture in the Person Drawing (Plate 111). It tells the viewer that Mary identifies with her mother, not as an abuser, but rather as a vulnerable female. Both figures are naked. Moreover, the female person has an open mouth attesting to her passivity and dependence. When we look at the male figure (Plate 112), we notice a pocket on his shirt. Pockets, which are seldom drawn by females, indicate maternal deprivation, a state often contributing to pathological tendencies (Urban, 1963). Since Mary identifies herself as a male, we can infer that this symbol mirrors her unmet dependency needs.

The feelings of weakness, dependence, and vulnerability are untenable for Mary to handle. Rather than letting herself be nakedly open to them, she chooses to identify with the more powerful male, which may, in fact, be a reaction formation. She drew the male figure first which is atypical (Gravitz, 1967). Generally, when this is done it signals a disturbance in sexual identity. When the opposite sex is drawn first, it is associated with conflict regarding sexual identification and is also linked to lesbian proclivity (Machover, 1980). This is not surprising, as early on Mary was cast into the role of her mother's man. The very fact that she drew a naked figure further portrays her sexual maladjustment.

Lorette

Lorette is a 30-year-old woman who graduated high school and is currently employed as a hairstylist. She is single and has no children. The memory of her sexual abuse is still somewhat repressed, despite three and a half years of therapy. The use of repression is a common defense mechanism employed by victims and often serves to maintain their ego integrity (Stafford-Clark, 1972). The trauma of the sexual desecration is so devastating that the eruption of the memory, even 15 years later—as in this case—threatens to disrupt to the survivor's functioning. As such, repression provides a protective purpose.

Although the memory may not be in the victim's conscious experience, the events that surround the molestation continue to exert their influence. Therefore, it is essential that the recollection of the sexual attack becomes conscious so that the survivor can understand his or her behavior and become in charge of his or her own actions. Currently, Lorette has been able to remember being sexually abused beginning sometime around the ages of 10 to 12. She believes the assault continued for five years. She is certain that her brother, who is five years older than she, violated her and feels that her father may have also done so. The abuse she is able to recall includes genital exposure, masturbation, fellatio, digital penetration of her vagina, penile penetration, and dry intercourse.

One of the most striking aspects in this series of drawings is Lorette's rendition of the Person (Plate 113), in which the only suggestions that an individual has been drawn are the detailed facial features. Most unusual is the fact that there is no definition outlining the face. It is as if the person becomes part of the paper. Since the paper, in a projective drawing, represents the

PLATE 113.

PLATE 114.

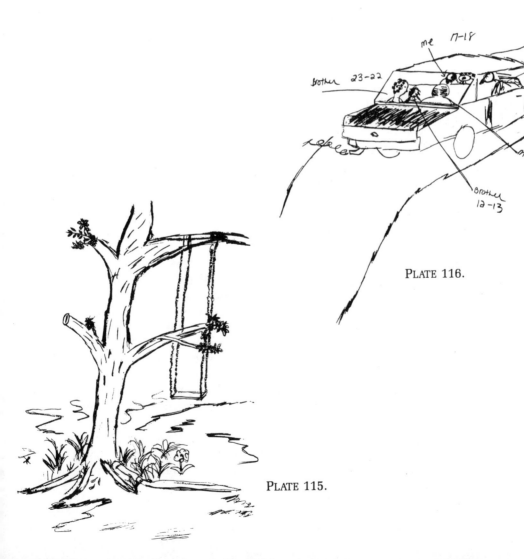

brother 23-22   me   17-18   Father

mother

brother
12-13

PLATE 116.

PLATE 115.

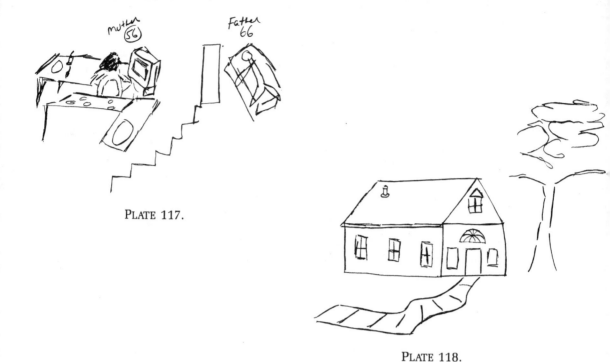

PLATE 117.

PLATE 118.

world, this rendering is a metaphor of Lorette's melding into the environment. The face is that part of our bodies through which we present ourselves to society. It may well be that Lorette becomes one with her environment and, as such, has developed a false self.

The Tree Drawing (see Plate 115), on the other hand, provides the viewer with information regarding Lorette's "real" self. The shaded outline of the trunk reflects Lorette's feelings of weakness and powerlessness. The heavy shading and reinforced outline also create a sense of emphasis, which projects her struggle to hold herself together. Lorette's feeling of impotence is also made evident by the omission of the body in her Person Drawings (Plates 113, 114). Although this exclusion implies her use of the defense mechanism of denial— she is repudiating her body drives—it is obvious that without one's body, one has no power.

This sense of helplessness originates, in large part, from being sexually molested while a child by one, if not two, family members. The sawed-off tree branches, which start below the midline of the trunk, suggest that repression was a primary defense mechanism that Lorette deployed beginning in her early teens. To remind the reader, the line of development of the tree, from bottom to top, parallels an individual's experienced development in time, with the base of the trunk representing early life and the top, the current time.

Further evidence of Lorette's troublesome past is given in the PDI in which she stated that the worst part of the drawing is that the tree's "roots are bumpy." This statement unconsciously suggests the roughness of her early years. The reality is that her childhood was not a smooth ride. In her KFD of her family of origin (Plate 116), Lorette has drawn her family in a car with her doing the driving. Again, she stated "there is a huge bump in the road." Put in the driver's seat at a young age, by being forced to satisfy adult needs, unrealistic expectations were made of her. Metaphorically, she had a huge, overwhelming, and overpowering hump to negotiate, which left her feeling inadequate, helpless, and powerless.

However, as an adult, we see that Lorette has been able to make strides. The two cut-off branches, which appear dead, have growth sprouting out at the extension and side, thereby suggesting that there is a sense of life and hopefulness. The swing also portrays a positive note. As a symbol of one's proclivity towards experimentation and a sense of ease in the world (Marzolf & Kirchner, 1972), it represents Lorette's desire to develop these parts of herself. Hanging off the top branch, it reflects her most current development. Sadly, a lower branch, representing earlier times, is still blocking her movement.

An area of concern is Lorette's view of the male, which she presents in profile (Plate 114). This position attests to her experience of men as evasive and oppositional (Machover, 1980). Of interest, are the two dripping phallic-like protrusions at the top of the head. Might these not represent the two men who molested her? A breakdown in Lorette's ego strength is seen in her presentation of her father (Plate 117) in the KFD of her current family. The phallic appendages are the only transparencies present in the six drawings and clearly reflect her anxiety and questioning of reality testing regarding her father. Note, also, that she has isolated him as a way of containing him. This compartmentalization, which is also evident in the KFD of her family of origin (Plate 116), is the item most frequently identified in our study of sexually abused children (see Chapter 2).

One final statement needs to be made about Lorette's feeling of trust in relation to others. Not surprisingly, this is an area of difficulty for her, and is seen in several of her drawings. The reinforced eaves of the House Drawing (Plate 118) imply her overly guarded attitude. Her trust disturbance is also reflected by the lack of a doorknob and the house's high placement on the page. Further testimony is presented in both KFDs, where virtually all the figures have their backs to the viewer. Happily, however, Lorette has not given up on relating to others as she continues in therapy, working to overcome her early trauma.

Peggy

Peggy is a 39-year-old incest survivor, who was raised in a middle-class home. She is a college graduate currently working in a laundromat as an attendant. Marriage and having a family have exacerbated Peggy's vulnerabilities, leading her to repeated suicide attempts and eventuating in several psychiatric hospitalizations. For most of the past five years, Peggy has been able to maintain herself in individual outpatient psychotherapy with the help of psychotropic medication. She has had only a few intermittent rehospitalizations.

Peggy's sexual assault was at the hands of a trusted male neighbor. From approximately the age of 8 until well into her teenage years, with her parents' encouragement, she would visit with him. It was during these stays that he forced numerous heinous sexual acts upon her. Not only did they involve his ramming his penis into her vagina, but also included urinating and defecating upon her. These assaults continued until she found the strength to refuse being with him. Feeling it was her own fault, and believing he was a nice man, she remained silent about these acts until she reached adulthood. Moreover, recently while in therapy, she unearthed a memory that her father also sexually abused her during preschool years.

PLATE 119.

PLATE 120.

PLATE 121.

PLATE 122.

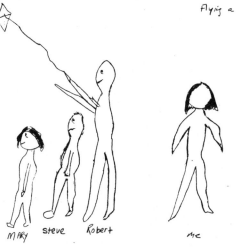

Flying a kite

MARY   steve   Robert   Me

PLATE 123.

There is a profound sense of emptiness that pervades Peggy's series of projective drawings. The face, as has been noted, is the most expressive part of the body and pivotal to verbal, as well as nonverbal, communication. Peggy presents the viewer with two figures in which she omits the facial features. In fact, hair is the only detail she allows in the Person Drawing (Plate 119). The absense of facial features (see also Plate 120) graphically expresses her use of avoidance as a major defense. Specifically, this treatment signifies the elusive manner in which she relates to others (Machover, 1980) and is sadly reminiscent of the colloquialism that refers to a blank or poker face in which all expressions are neutralized. In addition, there is a sense that Peggy would like to fade into the background as an anonymous figure or fade out completely as in her suicide attempts.

The suggestion of her evasiveness is carried into other drawings as well. The house (Plate 121), which is placed high on the page, connotes her desire to avoid environmental conflict and keep issues at bay. Likewise, in the Tree Drawing (Plate 122), we see the branches of the crown framed in a skin, portraying the artist's lack of communication. Within the skinlike shield are fear and embarrassment (Koch, 1952), which would be consistent with Peggy's history in which she felt that her abuser was "a nice man" and, she, paradoxically, was at fault.

Not only does Peggy avoid her inner life, but she also evades contact with others. This is projected by the lack of a pathway and the omission of ground-level windows in the House Drawing and the hands, hidden behind the back and out of sight, in both Person Drawings (Plates 119 & 120).

Interestingly, the action she selected for her KFD involves her husband and two children "flying a kite." It is as if she were telling them to get lost. Moreover, she also feels that others shy away her. They literally turn their backs on her in the KFD (Plate 123). The fact that Peggy feels very disconnected from others is further reflected in the branch structure of the tree. Some branches begin from nowhere and are connected to nothing. This sense of disconnection is echoed in the KFD where three members of her family are together flying a kite while Peggy stands uninvolved, alone, and poignantly faceless, merely taking up space.

Lisa

Twenty-eight-year-old Lisa is yet another victim of sexual abuse perpetrated by her father. She is hazy as to when these assaults began but is clear that they persisted for at least 15 years. The sexual activity ran the spectrum of sexual acts, bar none. She suspects that her mother was aware of the incidents but did not intercede on her behalf. In addition to the rapes, Lisa was also subjected to beatings and severe punishments, and also witnessed extreme violence in her family.

Lisa is married to an electrician. She graduated high school and is currently home raising her two children. She is grappling to master the aftermath of her long history of abuse. In the past she has had multiple addictions. To combat them she joined such support groups as Alcoholics Anonymous, Narcotics Anonymous, and Overeaters Anonymous. Recently, she has come to the realization that the source of her severe inner tension, dependency, and compulsivity are largely due to her traumatic childhood, most notably the incest. As such, she has joined an incest survivors group and has begun individual psychotherapy.

In viewing Lisa's six drawings, the line quality in five of them projects her anxiety, insecurity, and timidity. This is partially related to her feelings about bodily impulses. She clearly attempts to deny them by omitting the torso and limbs in the Person Drawings (Plates 124 & 125), reminiscent of the presentations created by two other adult survivors, Teressa and Lorette. Denial of sexual and aggressive impulses is a common scenario for victims of sexual abuse. Possibly because the genital stimulation during the abuse was pleasurable, or, conversely, because it was so unpleasant, the abused child seeks relief by denying the feelings. This means of coping, even though dysfunctional, becomes characteristic and then continues into adulthood.

Another defensive style Lisa had developed is intellectualization. Notice the elaborate, sophisticated representation of the heads and the focus on this body part (Levick, 1983). The House and the Tree Drawings (Plates 126 & 127, respectively) likewise reflect attention to detail and style. The emphasis on thought is further depicted by the presence of two roofs on the house. The lower roof, however, is shaded and has a transparency breaking through at the end wall. This suggests Lisa's overconcern about her thoughts, particularly in the area of fantasy. At times, the line between reality and fantasy becomes unclear and threatens her objectivity. She is struggling to stay bound to reality and to cap her fantasies, which is conveyed by the intensely shaded hair on both Person Drawings. Alternatively, these two roofs may raise concern as to a tendency to dissociate and literally separate her thoughts from each other.

An additional source of Lisa's anxiety is in regard to her feelings about men. The profile of the male figure (Plate 125) portrays her sense of male evasiveness. Additionally, the large obscured ear depicts her view that men are incapable of adequately hearing what she has to say. In the KFD of her family of origin (Plate 128), each male is again presented in profile, while the females are shown full face. Her father, also, holds a large fishing pole that extends beyond the paper. This represents her view of his power and contrasts dramatically with her portrayal of herself as small and lacking a body. Her anxiety about the male

PLATE 124.

PLATE 125.

PLATE 126.

PLATE 127.

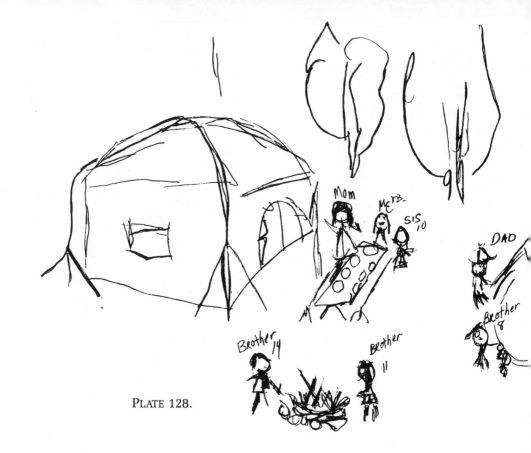

PLATE 128.

PLATE 129.

BEDTIME STORY

is further evident in the KFD of her current family (Plate 129), in which her husband is the only figure on the page with a transparency.

However, there is less agitation, in this KFD than in any other of Lisa's projective drawings, thereby suggesting that she has been able to develop a somewhat satisfying family life. This positive point is also echoed in her depiction of the tree (Plate 127). Notice that the roots on the lefthand side of the page are absent, while they are present on the right. Utilizing the concept that the past is represented on the page's left, we have a metaphor suggesting that Lisa feels more rooted in the present. Still and all, the aftermath of the abuse lingers as she is aligned with her daughter and her husband is compartmentalized with her son. This repeats the KFD of her family of origin (Plate 128), where the men and women are segregated and stay apart from each other, via their activities.

Although anxiety is a pervasive symptom from which Lisa suffers, depression also plagues her. This is dramatically revealed by her choice of a weeping willow as a tree (Hammer, 1980). Because the depiction of the tree is less susceptible to change over time (Hammer, 1980), it is safe to assume that this depression not only has a long history, but also will probably be more enduring than other problems. As depicted through the extended twisted branches, it is difficult for Lisa to secure satisfaction from the environment, although she tries. The branches do reach out towards the surroundings, conveying that she has not given up on others and still hopes for caring and support.

Glenda

Forty-nine-year-old Glenda is a divorced woman with four children. She was 5 years old the first time her father approached her sexually. His sexual behavior escalated during the next six years from initial genital exposure and culminated with vaginal intercourse. As time progressed, he began to threaten Glenda by pointing a knife at her, intimating he would kill her if she did not comply with his demands. Glenda experienced herself as being constantly terrorized and in horror of dying. Her mother was aware of the distorted relationship existing between her husband and daughter but felt helpless in stopping it. Although this living nightmare ended 38 years ago, Glenda is still plagued by its impact. She has been in therapy for the past eight years, attempting to undo the wake of damage wrought by her father's stream of assaults.

An important feature in Glenda's drawings is the line quality. In her House Drawing (Plate 130), Tree Drawing (Plate 131), Person Drawing 1 (Plate 132), Person Drawing 2 (Plate 133), and Kinetic Family Drawing of her current family (Plate 134) the line quality is unusually faint. (These drawings were so light that they required darkening in order to be reproduced for this book.) This suggests that Glenda feels inadequate and insecure, unable to make her mark on the environment. By contrast, in the Kinetic Family Drawing of her family of origin (Plate 135), the lines are much more intense and pressured, so much so that their imprint is seen through the back of the paper. Because they are heavy only in the specific drawing, we can conclude that Glenda has many unresolved issues in relation to her early family life.

PLATE 130.

PLATE 131.

PLATE 132.

PLATE 133.

Glenda's forceful lines on the KFD 2 intimate the hostility and accompanying anxiety she feels towards her childhood family (Jolles, 1971). Her family, as described in her PDI, is sitting down to eat, yet they are represented in stick form, thereby indicating Glenda's distaste for these relationships (Jolles, 1971). Strikingly, this rendering is cluttered with indicators of sexual abuse. In fact, the total composition of the figures, plates, and table are the sexually symbolic wedges and circles (Sidun & Rosenthal, 1987), which are not seen quite as dramatically elsewhere in this series.

Glenda's House Drawing does contain a few circles and wedges and also has one window significantly different from the others, the latter of which is a marker of probable incest (Cohen & Phelps, 1985). The four expansive windows represent her feelings of vulnerability, as they are uncovered and suggest that the house is defenselessly exposed. Perhaps this implies that Glenda, who gives us all the expected details, does a good job offering what one would want.

However, her anxiety about really letting anyone become close to her is reflected by the entryway treatment. Attention is drawn to the door by the two windows and the scribbled doorknob. How one would open the door, though, is confusing. In addition, for a pathway to offer accessibility it needs to be open at the entrance and relatively wide where one would first step onto it. In a drawing rendition, it normally becomes narrower towards the door. The fact that Glenda presents the opposite is a possible confirmation that she hesitates to let others make contact with her.

The drawing of her current family (Plate 134) depicts Glenda and her children having a talk after a holiday meal. However, the configuration of the four figures implies just how removed Glenda feels from others. The children are all seated together, while she is laid out on the floor beside them almost ready to be stepped upon. Like the KFD of her family of origin, she is also the smallest person, which conveys her poor self-esteem.

Glenda attempts to compensate for her feelings of powerlessness and impotence. This can be seen in her drawing of a tree, which takes up the entire page and appears to need even more space. The large size of this image strongly suggests that Glenda tends to overcompensate against feeling small and weak. This defense is also apparent when comparing the sizes of the female and male Person Drawings. In her PDI she identifies the female as a self-portrait and the male as her father. The woman is at least twice the size of the man, and although he raped her at knifepoint for over six years, she draws herself as the larger and, therefore, more powerful person. Unfortunately, Glenda never had the opportunity while growing up to feel powerful or in charge of herself. Based on her history, we know that she was never given the opportunity to have a normally dependent relationship through which she might have gained a sense of strength, competency, and independence.

Glenda attempts to mitigate against her yet unsatisfied dependency needs are projected through the broad base of the tree's trunk (Levine & Sapolsky, 1969), the buttons on the woman's dress (Plate 132) and Glenda's open mouth in the KFD 1. These yet unmet needs have resulted in her becoming a somewhat self-absorbed adult who tries desperately to give to herself. The weeping willow tree not only portrays her depression, but also mirrors how she enfolds

PLATE 134.

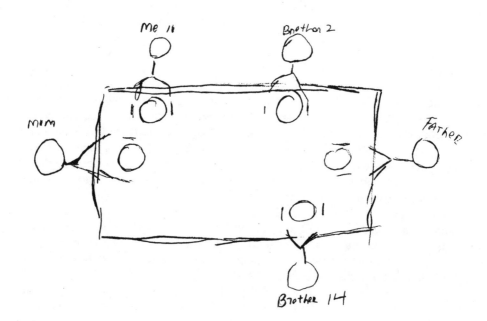

PLATE 135.

herself. The branches seem to embrace the trunk rather than reach outward into the surroundings. This self-absorption is further reflected by the balanced stance of the tree (Koch, 1952). Similarly, in her PDI, she describes the female person as "holding herself." Note that the eyes have no pupils, another indication of her self-involvement (Levine & Sapolsky, 1969). Plates 131 and 132 portray her need to provide the self-care from which she was deprived and which has resulted in narcissistic self-absorption.

Melanie

Melanie, a forty-two-year-old woman who has never married, received both her bachelor and master's degrees from college. She is currently employed as a full-time printer. Melanie fell victim to her father's sexual impulses. Both Melanie and her sister, who is eight years younger, were the prey of their father. He introduced them to a full range of sexual activity, excluding only cunnilingus and fellatio. For Melanie, the exploitation began when she was 6 years old and continued until she was 12. Despite the long length of time during which abuse continued, her mother seemed oblivious to it. At the time of this writing, Melanie had been in psychotherapy for six and a half years and in an incest support group for one year. In spite of her efforts to come to terms with the aftermath of the abuse, scars remain and mar her self-perception, as can be seen in the drawings that follow.

The sexual abuse that went on throughout Melanie's latency years set the stage for her identification. Having experienced life as a victim in her early years, she came to believe, on some level of consciousness, that being the male and the aggressor was a more preferable position. Both Person Drawings, as well as her rendering in the Tree Drawing, reflect her identification with the male aggressor as a defense mechanism.

In the first Person Drawing (Plate 136), she draws a male figure rather than a person of her own sex. This portrayal of the opposite sex as her initial Person Drawing symbolizes her identification with the man, the person who aggressed her. This hostility is further projected by the clenched and angry position of the hands in the Person of the Opposite Sex Drawing (Plate 137). The sharp branches emanating from all sides of the tree (Plate 138) also reflect this trait (Koch, 1952). It is most pronounced, however, by her selection of a seaman as the persona for the first drawing. A sailor is an individual professionally trained to be assaultive. By this choice she has sublimated her hostile drives into a socially acceptable path.

Noteworthy is the phallic symbolism in Melanie's first Person Drawing. The heavily shaded, long and pointed tie and the shaded beard represent her emphasis and anxiety in relation to the penis. Furthermore, a double entendre is implied in her selection of a "seaman," which is pronounced the same as "semen." Even the person she drew of "the opposite sex" looks like a man, additionally conveying her strong identification with male sexuality. Melanie's effort to harness and control sexual and aggressive impulses is depicted by placing the sailor's tie within a fabric flap, literally restraining this seaman.

When one studies her Kinetic Family Drawing 1 (Plate 139), Melanie's image of a female becomes painfully clear. Notice that her mother is the only person

"A Person"   "A Person of the Opposite Sex"

PLATE 136.   PLATE 137.

A US Navy Seaman   1959

1959

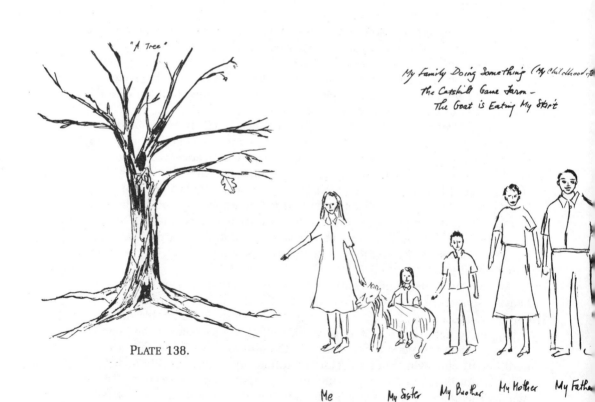

"A Tree"

My Family Doing Something (My Childhood at
the Catskill Game Farm —
The Goat is Eating My Skirt

PLATE 138.

Me   My Sister   My Brother   My Mother   My Father
14   6   9   34   39

PLATE 139.

1957

My Family Doing Something (Current Family)

Me

My Sister
My Brother-in-Law
My Nephew (4)

My Brother
My Sister-in-Law
My Step-Niece
(6)

My Mother My Father

PLATE 140.

"A House"

1950

PLATE 141.

without a neck. The head seems to be floating above her body, disconnected and off center. It is as if Melanie sees her mother as an "air head" with little substance or ability to make connections. Her "still innocent" sister (Melanie's words from the PDI) needs to be protected; her vulnerable genitals are hidden by the goat. Melanie's sense of her own defenselessness within the context of the family is clearly present as expressed by the goat eating her skirt.

The House Drawing (Plate 141) also projects Melanie's discomfort within her family. It is far away and, as such, depicts her feeling that comforts are out of reach in relation to those at home (Hammer, 1980). The peculiarly placed tree in this drawing, which may represent Melanie, likely conveys her strong feelings of rejection coupled with an intense need for connectedness and love from her family members (Buck, 1981). Significantly, the tree appears attached, almost growing out of the roof, representing Melanie's link to her family. Interestingly, shrubs often represent siblings, of which Melanie has two. In this drawing there is a shrub on each side of the house.

Melanie's inability to separate from her family, even at age 42, is most likely due to her unmet dependency needs. This experience is implied by the buttons and pockets present in her Person of the Opposite Sex Drawing (Plate 137), which Melanie identified as herself. Additionally, in discussing the drawing of the sailor (Plate 136), she stated that she liked his independence. The sailor seems to represent her ego ideal and trait towards which she strides.

Melanie does not feel strong enough to stand on her own two feet (note size and shading of feet in Plates 136 and 137), as there is a pervasive sense of inner barrenness and a perceived lack of inner resources. The tree (Plate 138) appears almost lifeless, with a tiny acorn and one leaf as the only suggestions of life. The positive note is that the branches on the right side of the page appear to extend more fully out into the world. It is also only on this side, the area associated with the future, that foliage appears to represent hope and potential growth.

Sadly we must add a caveat. As long as Melanie is able to separate from the noxious pressure of her family and reach out into the environment—as she does in the Tree Drawing—she has the possibility of flourishing. However, if she remains trapped within the confines of the family's pathology, she is at risk of disintegration. In fact, Melanie is aware of this at some level, for she states in her PDI of the Kinetic Family Drawing 2 (Plate 140) that "we are all splintered—no one is sure of themselves. . . ." The metaphor is graphically portrayed. The family obliterates her sense of self.

Dorothy

Twenty-two-year-old Dorothy was molested by a trusted adult and family friend. In Dorothy's case it was her priest. Her family's relationship with their clergyman was close; the priest spent two summers living with the family at their summer home. During these months the priest would take Dorothy and her younger sister for country drives. The seating in the car was always the same. Dorothy sat in the back, her sister in the front. While he was driving, Father O'Reilly would engage in what became a predictable occurrence; he would extend his hand into the backseat and reach up Dorothy's dress. There

PLATE 142.

PLATE 143.

PLATE 144.

PLATE 145.

PLATE 146.

were also times when he would take both girls to the beach and fondle them in the water. Sadly, Dorothy is a multiple victim. When she was 8, an old man touched her and that same year a teenage cousin put his finger inside her vagina. Dorothy tried to tell her parents about the abuses, but they did not believe her.

Dorothy stated that she always felt left out of the family. She described her parents as distant and involved in a great deal of marital tension. Her father is a pilot and a recovering alcoholic. When Dorothy was 15, she became agoraphobic and could no longer attend school. Tutors came to her home and she was able to graduate from high school with honors. At age 17 she was psychiatrically hospitalized due to a worsening of the agoraphobia. She was also suffering from panic attacks and somatic complaints and had periods of depersonalization. During the course of her hospitalization, she made a decision to report the priest to the Catholic church. Church officials found her story credible and Father O'Reilly was deported. Currently, Dorothy is in outpatient treatment but is still virtually housebound. Moreover, she cannot be left at home alone without enduring undue distress.

Because of her life events, Dorothy has developed a rigid character structure to help control the strong impulses aroused in her by the sexual molestations. Her ego is, in a sense, underfunctioning while her rigid superego predominates her psyche. The term rigidity, which is thought of colloquially as a stiff body posture, is pictorially represented by the upper bodies in both of Dorothy's Person Drawings (Plates 142 & 143). The squared-off chests and arms pressed to the sides reflect Dorothy's constricted ego and inflexible superego (Ogdon, 1977). These same characteristics are seen in the rulerlike lines that appear to box in the House Drawing (Plate 144) (Jolles, 1971).

Underneath Dorothy's stilted personality organization she holds in hostile inclinations and sexual impulses. This is projected throughout several of her drawings. The squared-off shoulders (Plates 142 & 143) mirror her underlying anger. Her concealed, intense sexual impulses are portrayed by the enlarged nose, the designed skirt hiding the genitalia of the female figure, and the outline of the crotch on Dorothy's self-portrait in the KFD (Plate 145). The brickwork encasing the large, detailed chimney in the House Drawing (Plate 144) also reflects her latent sexual drives. Likewise, the tremulous lines delineating the tree crown (Plate 146) depict her inhibitions (Koch, 1952).

Both Dorothy's impulses and real self are disconnected from her sense of self. This is graphically depicted by the opposing lines within the crown of the tree (Koch, 1952) and reflective of Krystal's concept of alexithymia wherein one becomes removed from one's own feelings, virtually dead to emotions. In fact, when we look at the other drawings in this group, particularly the House, and even the KFD, a sense of deadness and estrangement pervades.

This demonstrates that Dorothy has detached herself from feelings and repressed her impulses. It is, therefore, not surprising that she has developed a phobia as a means of coping with her overwhelming drives. She literally remains tightly confined by rigid walls, because the outside world is boundless and cannot provide the contraints necessary for her to contain her impulses. The House Drawing, situated high on the page, demonstrates that Dorothy is not only afraid of herself, but also fears the environment (Landisberg, 1969).

It is also worth noting that in the wound in the tree trunk there is a sensation of one circle containing another, thereby offering successive layers of protection. This virtually duplicates Dorothy's agoraphobia and helps explain her ongoing need to remain at home. It is almost as if Dorothy requires constant reassurance that she will be safeguarded. However, notice the umbrella (Plate 145) that stands above her parents. Although umbrellas generally afford protection, this one is tenuously staked in the ground and doesn't even cast a shadow against the sun's rays. Apparently, in Dorothy's experience, no one in her family is protected from the elements of the outside world.

Another scar sustained by Dorothy as a result of the sexual abuse is related to her sense of her own body. Body joints, which are most pronounced in the KFD, are also present in the male and female Person Drawings. Ogdon (1977) states that the presence of joints is a rarity. Their inclusion, therefore, implies Dorothy's uncertainty about the intactness of her body. This is a frequent aftermath of sexual abuse, for many victims experience themselves as damaged.

Dorothy's KFD provides the viewer with additional insights about her experience of family life. In her drawing of the family at a beach, she portrays everyone involved in a seemingly pleasurable activity. In reality, the beach is one of the landscapes of her sexual abuse. Just as her family remained passive during the course of her victimization, she depicts them in this drawing as standing by the water "watching," doing little else. Notice that the two men have their hands in their pockets, emphasizing their placid stance in not protecting her and almost a relaxed, loafing attitude. That Dorothy wishes for a more stable and strong family, however, is suggested by the dark and overly long baseline of the House Drawing.

Elizabeth

Elizabeth, a 36-year-old woman who grew up in an alcoholic home, is married with three children. She graduated from college and works part-time. She is in individual therapy, in an incest survivors support group, and has been a participant in groups for adult children of alcoholics.

Elizabeth thinks that her father started to sexually abuse her when she was 6 and continued for a few years. Many of the details are still repressed, but she is able to recall digital vaginal penetration, as well as her father rubbing his penis against her genital area. Although she is uncertain as to whether her mother knew about the abuse, she felt her mother was emotionally absent. Because many of her memories have not yet surfaced, Elizabeth experiences many symptoms she does not understand. In fact, she stated that she does feel "not in control of her existence."

The ego function of regulating her impulses, her affects, and her life is a core issue for Elizabeth. This theme runs throughout most of her drawings. The House Drawing (Plate 147) presents the viewer with very little except the bare essentials. In this way, Elizabeth controls the information she reveals about herself. More unusual is the line that separates the second floor from the main level. This rarely seen delineation of the upstairs from the downstairs may metaphorically represent Elizabeth's attempt to compartmentalize and limit interaction on two levels. In addition, as seen in many other victims' drawings, it implies the use of dissociation.

First is her effort to curtail familial contact; second is her struggle to repress unacceptable parts of herself. However, this defense is not effective, for a close examination of the drawing reveals multiple erasures in the roof (these erasures are not visible in this reproduction). In fact, the line separating the roof from the main body of the house has gaps in its continuity, a result of these erasures, signifying Elizabeth's conflictual feelings about her thoughts and fantasies.

Control issues are also graphically connoted in her drawing of a female person (Plate 148). Note the elongated neck and striped belt. Both of these items are associated with difficulty in controlling basic drives and impulses (Buck, 1973; Levy, 1950). The pressure of Elizabeth's drives are strong and unacceptable to her. Another way that she attempts to cope with the anxiety that they arouse is through compulsive defenses. These are depicted in the striped shirt of the female figure, the uniformity and detail in the KFD 1 (Plate 150) and the ruffles on the bed in KFD 2 (Plate 151) (Hammer, 1954; Machover, 1949).

Elizabeth's excessive use of defenses to block her anxiety leads to confused thinking. The scribbled tree crown (Plate 152) and the scribbled hair on the female (Plate 148) both attest to this problem. In addition, there are numerous transparencies in this series of drawings that show a break in her reality testing. The most apparent of these are seen in the feet of the two Person Drawings (Plates 148 & 149). The feet are literally the area that comes into contact with the real world. They are the way through which we ground ourselves and maintain stability. This is the area where Elizabeth's reality shows the most serious breakdown.

PLATE 147.

PLATE 148.

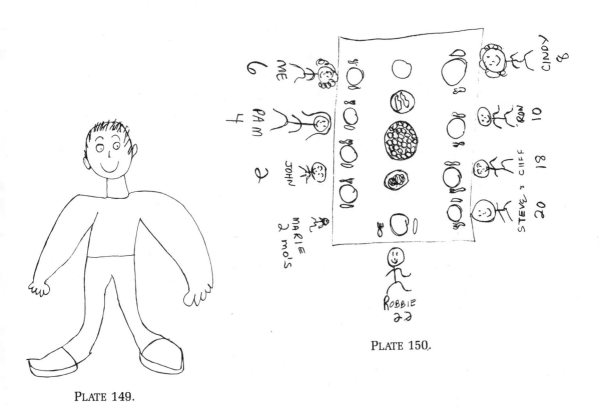

ME 6
PAM 4
JOHN 2
MARIE 2 mo's

CINDY 8
RON 10
STEVE & CLIFF 18
20
ROBBIE 22

PLATE 149.

PLATE 150.

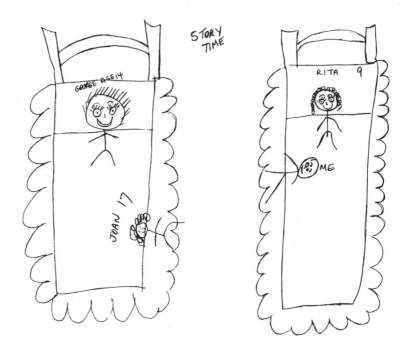

PLATE 151.

PLATE 152.

The place where Elizabeth loses the most perspective is within the context of her family of origin (Plate 150). When viewing this drawing its direction is unclear. No matter which way the viewer holds the picture, someone is always upside down. Perhaps this reflects the lack of direction the children in Elizabeth's family experienced in not knowing which was the correct way. Note that her parents are not even included in the drawing. Literally out of the picture, they leave the children to fend for themselves. But, the youngsters do not fend well for themselves, for no one faces the food at this Thanksgiving meal. This inability to know "which end is up" continues to plague Elizabeth in the present. In the KFD 2 (Plate 151), she appears to be floating on her side, still ungrounded and lacking a sense of the "correct" way.

The memory of her early childhood evokes considerable anxiety for Elizabeth and causes her to regress. The members in the KFD 1 are all portrayed through stick figures, which are a more primitive representation than the figures in her Person drawings. This may also symbolize her feelings of shame about her family and family life. Of particular note is the presence of beds in her KFD 2. Burns and Kaufman (1972) report that the appearance of beds in a Kinetic Family Drawing is extremely unusual and suggests sexualization or depression. Even more exceptional, and therefore more meaningful, is when everyone in the drawing is drawn in bed.

CONCLUSION

The authors find it distinctive that of the 10 adult survivors presented in this chapter, five or 50 percent included beds in their KFDs. In addition, a significant portion of these women sketched their KFDs in a cruder and more elementary form than their other projective drawings. These two characteristics may warrant further investigation to assess if they are a statistically significant index of previous sexual abuse.

Nevertheless, the presence of a bed in a KFD, as well as the quality of the presentation of family members, bear noting when a projective series is given. Further research is needed to glean other quantitative indices to help alert the clinician to an early history of sexual victimization. However, as this chapter clearly demonstrates, qualitative analysis of the drawings of adult survivors enables the examiner to gain access to information about the function of the ego, superego, and quality of object relations that otherwise may not be readily apparent.

A SURVIVOR'S LETTER

"An Open Letter to My Children"

Where do I begin? To talk about myself, or rather my childhood, is very painful; writing about it is even more difficult. How do I explain to my children my growing up years — years filled with terror, hate, and love. How can I explain the absolute fear that I lived with every waking moment.

While I do not remember my childhood in detail, I have always remembered enough about the sexual, psychological, and physical abuse to know that I am not imagining it. I lived in a home with a mother who was narcissistic, ruling the house through terror, arrogance, and manipulation. It was not enough to endure the most intimate sexual acts, but I could even be beaten for the smallest infraction of the rules. I barely remember my father before the age of 12. His way of dealing with me was to not talk to me for weeks on end. I could never tell anyone about the sexual abuse, because it was a subject never discussed and not even written about, except in fiction.

Add to the beatings, silent treatment, and sexual abuse a picture of being told constantly that you are dumb — "it's a shame your brother got all the brains and you're stupid." Constant ridicule. "You're so dumb, you can't even pass a test." In a way they are right. I was so dumb that I believed everything they told me. Like, "Don't tell anyone what goes on in our house — it's private." And I fell for it. Dumb — Dumb.

Then your mother, who was never allowed to be a child, gave birth to her first child. But if I was never a child, how could I be a mother? When they put my oldest son in my arms for the first time, all I could think about was, "Please God, don't let me be like her." With that for a foundation I entered motherhood. I repeated the same prayer each time one of you was born. How could I bring up children to understand boundaries, discipline, and guidelines, when I had never known them? How could I teach that which I had never learned? It was a little like treading water, and I had to tread very fast just to stay afloat.

As a child I was never allowed to express anger; as an adult I still have trouble expressing myself. Yes, I could yell at you children just as I was yelled at, but yelling is one thing — expressing yourself is quite another.

Another thing I am just learning to do is to ask for help. As a child of 6 I asked my mother for help when I told her about the sexual abuse I had endured. When she did nothing, I learned very early that I couldn't ask for help. There would be none given. Now I am just learning to ask for help; and yes sometimes you all say no, and that's alright too—I just have to learn to ask again.

There are so many things in my past that are hard to explain. I think you can understand the dependency and helplessness of a child for her parents—now try to understand how I felt when those very people to whom I turned for love, care, and affection abused me. Can you begin to understand the fear that became a part of my life? No child can really hate his or her parents because these are the people that you depend on to take care of you. If you can't hate them and you really can't love them, then you have a hard time as an adult trying to sort out your feelings of love and hate.

I am fortunate to be a part of the Themis Society, an organization dedicated to providing a safe and supportive environment for victims of childhood sexual abuse. A place where you go from a victim to a survivor. A place where you not only learn to nurture yourself, but also where you discover a new family who feels your pain and supports your growth. A place where there are no more secrets. I am still amazed that I am able to go out and give speeches about the effects of childhood sexual abuse on adults and even more amazed when people come up to thank me for my assistance in helping them understand this illness. My only regret is that none of you have ever expressed a desire to hear me speak.

I could only hope that through this letter your understanding of me might be a little better, a little clearer, a little more compassionate. I love all of you very much. No mother could be prouder of her children and what they have accomplished than I am of you.

With all my love always,

Mom

EMILY LIPMAN
President, Themis Society

BIBLIOGRAPHY

Abbele, F. (1970). *Interpretazioni psicologiche del disegno infantile.* Florence: Edizioni OS.

Albright, A., & Reice, (1986). Psychiatric aspects of sexual abuse. *Bulletin of the American Academy of Psychiatry, Law,* 14(4), 331–343.

Alschuler, A., & Hattwick, W. (1947). *Painting and Personality.* Chicago, IL: University of Chicago Press.

The American Heritage Dictionary of the English Language (1981). Morris, W. (Ed.). Boston, MA: Houghton Mifflin Co.

American Psychiatric Association. (1987). *Diagnostic and statistical manual of mental disorders, third edition, revised.* Washington, DC: American Psychiatric Press.

Arieti, S. (1976). *Creativity: The magic synthesis.* New York: Basic Books, Inc.

Bender, L. (1952). *Child psychiatric techniques.* Springfield, IL: Charles C Thomas.

Bender, L., & Blau, A. (1937). The reaction of children to sexual relations with adults. *American Journal of Orthopsychiatry,* 7, 825–837.

Blain, G., Bergner, R., Lewis, M., & Goldstein, M. (1981). The use of objectively scorable House-Tree-Person indicators to establish child abuse. *The Journal of Clinical Psychology,* 37(3), 667–673.

Bowen, M. (1978). *Family therapy and clinical practice.* New York: Jason Aronson.

Bresee, P., Stearns, G., Bess, B., & Packer, L. (1986). Allegations of child sexual abuse in child custody disputes: A therapeutic assessment model. *American Journal of Orthopsychiatry,* 56(4), 560–569.

Briere, J., & Runtz, M. (1987). Post-sexual abuse trauma. Data and implications for clinical practice. *Journal of Interpersonal Violence,* 2(4), 367–379.

Brooks B. (1985). Sexually abused children and adolescent identity development. *American Journal of Psychotherapy,* 39(3), 401–411.

Brothers, D. (1982). Trust disturbances among rape and incest victims. (Doctoral dissertation, Yeshiva University, 1982). *Dissertation Abstracts International,* 1247, 43(4-B).

Browne, A., & Finkelhor, D. (1986). Impact of child sexual abuse: A review of the research. *Psychological Bulletin,* 99(1), 66–77.

Buck, J. (1947). *The House-Tree-Person Test.* Richmond, Virginia: Colony.

Buck, J. (1948). The H-T-P technique, a qualitative and quantitative scoring manual. *Journal of Clinical Psychology,* 4, 317–396.

Buck, J. (1950). The use of the H-T-P test in a case of marital discord. *Journal of Projective Techniques,* 14, 405–434.

Buck, J. (1951). Quality of the quantity of the H-T-P. *Journal of Clinical Psychology,* 7, 352–356.

Buck, J. (1966). *The House-Tree-Person Technique: Revised Manual.* Los Angeles, CA: Western Psychological Services.

Buck, J. (1973). *The House-Tree-Person Technique: Revised Manual.* Los Angeles, CA: Western Psychological Services.

Buck, J. (1980). The H-T-P, a measure of adult intelligence. Lynchburg State Colony Virginia, 1947 (mimeographed manual) in *The Clinical Application of Projective Drawings.* Springfield, IL: Charles C Thomas.

Buck, J. (1981). *The House-Tree-Person Technique: Revised Manual.* Los Angeles, CA: Western Psychological Services.

Buckley, P. (1986). *Essential Papers on Object Relations.* New York & London: New York University Press.

Burgess, A., McCausland, M., & Wolbert, W. (1981). Children's drawings as indicators of sexual trauma. *Perspectives in Psychiatric Care, 19*(2) 50-58.

Burns, R., & Kaufman, S. H. (1972). *Actions, Styles and Symbols in Kinetic Family Drawings (K-F-D). An Interpretative Manual.* New York: Brunner/Mazel.

Burt, C. (1921). *Mental and Scholastic Tests.* London: P.S. King & Son.

Butler, S. (1978). *Conspiracy of Silence.* New York: Bantam Books.

Chess, S., & Hassibi, M. (1981). *Principles and Practice of Child Psychiatry.* New York: Plenum Press.

Chranowski, G. (1978). Comments and Criticisms. Malevolent Transformation and the negative therapeutic reaction. *Contemporary Psychoanalysis, 14*(3), 405-415.

Cohen, B., & Cox, C. (1989). Breaking the code: Identification of multiplicity through art productions. *Dissociation, 2*(3) 132-137.

Cohen, F., & Phelps, R. (1985). Incest markers in children's artwork. *The Arts in Psychotherapy, 12,* 265-383.

Cohen, T. (1983). The incestuous family revisited. *Social Casework: The Journal of Contemporary Social Work, March,* 154-161.

Coons, P. (1986). Child abuse and multiple personality disorders: Review of the literature and suggestions for treatment. *Child Abuse and Neglect. The International Journal, 10*(4), 455-462.

Demers-Desrosiers, L. (1982). Influence of alexithymia on symbolic function. *Psychotherapy Psychosomatics, 38,* 103-120.

Di Leo, J. (1970). *Young Children and Their Drawings.* New York: Brunner/Mazel.

Di Leo, J. (1973). *Children's Drawings as Diagnostic Aids.* New York: Brunner/Mazel.

Di Leo, J. (1983). *Interpreting Children's Drawings.* New York: Brunner/Mazel.

Erikson, E. H. (1963). *Childhood and Society.* New York: W. W. Norton & Co.

Eth, S., & Pynoos, R. (1985). *Post-Traumatic Stress Disorder in Children.* Washington, DC: American Psychiatric Press.

Everstine, D. S., & Everstine, L. (1989). *Sexual Trauma in Children and Adolescents: Dynamics and Treatment.* New York: Brunner/Mazel.

Fairbairn, W. (1952). *Psychoanalytic Studies of the Personality.* London: Routledge, Kegan & Paul.

Ferenczi, S. (1949). Confusion of tongues between the adult and the child. (The language of tenderness and of passion). *International Journal of Psychoanalysis, 30,* 225-230.

Finkelhor, D. (1986). *A Sourcebook on Child Sexual Abuse.* Beverly Hills, CA: Sage Publications.

Finkelhor, D., & Browne, A. (1985). The traumatic impact of child sexual abuse: A conceptualization. *American Journal of Orthopsychiatry, 55*(4), 530-541.

Finkelhor, D., Hotaling, G., Lewis, I. A., & Smith, C. (1989). Sexual abuse and its relationship to later sexual satisfaction, marital status, religion and attitudes. *Journal of Interpersonal Violence, 4* (4), 379-399.

Forward, S., & Buck, C. (1978). *Betrayal of Innocence.* Middlesex, England: Penguin Books.

Freud, A. (1952). The role of bodily illness in the mental life of children. *The Psychoanalytic Study of the Child, 7,* 69-81. New York: International Universities Press.

Freud, A. (1965). *Normality and Pathology in Childhood.* New York: International Universities Press.

Freud, A. (1966). *The Ego and the Mechanisms of Defense.* New York: International Universities Press.

Freud, A. (1982). A psychoanalyst's view of sexual abuse by parents. In P. B. Mrazek & C. H. Kempe (Eds.), *Sexually Abused Children and Their Families.* New York: Pergamon Press.

Freud, S. (1957). Mourning and melancholia. In J. Strachey (Ed. and Trans.), *The Standard Edition of the Complete Works of Sigmund Freud* (Vol. 14). London: Hogarth Press. (Original work published 1917)

Freud, S. (1959). Inhibitions, symptoms, and anxiety. In J. Strachey (Ed. and Trans.), *The Standard Edition of the Complete Works of Sigmund Freud* (Vol. 20, pp. 75-175). London: Hogarth Press. (Original work published 1926)

Freud, S., & Breuer, J. (1955). Studies on hysteria. In J. Strachey (Ed. and Trans.), *The Standard Edition of the Complete Works of Sigmund Freud* (Vol. 2). London: Hogarth Press. (Original work published 1893-1895)

Fromuth, M. E. (1983). *The long-term psychological impact of childhood sexual abuse.* Unpublished doctoral disseration, Auburn University.

Furst, S. (1967). *Psychic Trauma.* New York: Basic Books.

Geiser, R. (1979). *Hidden Victims.* Boston: Beacon Press.

Gelinas D. (1983). The persisting negative effects of incest. *Psychiatry, 46*(Nov.), 312-332.

Gravitz, M. A. (1967). Marital status and figure drawing choice in normal adults. *Journal of Projective Techniques and Personality Assessment, 31,* 86-87.

Greenberg, J., & Mitchell, S. (1983). *Object Relations in Psychoanalytic Theory.* Massachusetts: Harvard University Press.

Griffiths, R. (1935). *A Study of Imagination in Early Childhood.* London: Kegan Paul, Trench, Trubner & Company.

Groth, N., Hobson, W., & Gary, T. (1982) The child molester: Clinical observations. In J. R. Conte & D. A. Shore (Eds.), *Social Work and Child Sexual Abuse.* New York: The Haworth Press.

Gurvitz, M. (1951). *The Dynamics of Psychological Testing.* New York: Grune & Stratton.

Haley, J. (1976). *Problem Solving Therapy.* San Francisco: Jossey-Bass.

Hammer, E. (1953). An investigation of sexual symbolism: A study of the HTP'S of eugenically sterilized subjects. *Journal of Projective Techniques, 17,* 401-413.

Hammer, E. (1954). Guide for qualitative research with the H-T-P. *Journal of General Psychology, 51,* 41-60.

Hammer, E. (1968). *The Clinical Application of Projective Drawings.* Springfield, IL: Charles C Thomas.

Hammer, E. (1968). Projective Drawings. In Al Rabin (Ed.), *Projective Techniques in Personality Assessment* (pp. 366-393). New York: Springer.

Hammer, E. (1980). *The Clinical Application of Projective Drawings.* Springfield, IL: Charles C Thomas.

Harris, D. (1963). *Children's Drawings as Measures of Intellectual Maturity.* New York: Harcourt Brace Jovanovich, Inc.

Hartmann, H. (1954). *Notes on the theory of sublimation.* Presentation at the American Psychoanalytic Association, New York.

Herman, J., Russell, D., & Trocki, K. (1986). Long-term effects of incestuous abuse in childhood. *American Journal of Psychiatry, 143*(10), 1293-1296.

Hibbard, R., Roghmann, K., & Hoekelman, R. (1987). Genitalia in children's drawings: An association with sexual abuse. *Pediatrics, 79*(1), 129-137.

Hillman, D., & Solek-Tefft, J. (1988). *Spiders and Flies: Help for Parents and Teachers of Sexually Abused Children.* Springfield, MA: Lexington Books.

Hoffman, L. (1981). *Foundations of Family Therapy.* New York: Basic Books.

Jacobson, E. (1954). The Self and the Object World. *Psychoanalytic Study of the Child, 9,* 75-127. New Haven: Yale University Press.

James, J., & Meyerding, J. (1977). Early sexual experience and prostitution. *American Journal of Psychiatry, 134:* 1381-1385.

Jolles, I. (1952). *A Catalogue for the Qualitative Interpretation of the HTP.* Beverly Hills, CA: Western Psychological Services.

Jolles, I. (1964). *A Catalogue for the Qualitative Interpretation of the HTP.* Beverly Hills, CA: Western Psychological Services.

Jolles, I. (1971). *A Catalogue for the Qualitative Interpretation of the H-T-P. (Revised).* Los Angeles, CA: Western Psychological Services.

Justice, B. & R. (1979). *The Broken Taboo.* New York: Human Sciences Press.

Katan, A. (1973). Children who were raped. *Psychoanalytic Study of the Child, 28,* 208–224. New Haven: Yale University Press.

Kaufman, I., Peck A., & Tagiuri C. K. (1954). The family constellation and overt incestuous relations between father and daughter. *American Journal of Orthopsychiatry, 24,* 266–277.

Kelley, S. (1981). Children's drawings as indicators of sexual trauma. *Perspectives in Psychiatric Care, 11*(2), 50–58.

Kelley, S. (1984). The use of art therapy with the sexually abused child. *Journal of Psychosocial Nursing and Mental Health Services, 22*(12), 12–18.

Kelley, S. (1985). Drawings: Critical communications for sexually abused children. *Pediatric Nursing, 11,* 421–426.

Kellogg, R. (1969). *Analyzing Children's Art.* Palo Alto, CA: Mayfield Publishing Company.

Kellogg, R. (1970). *Analyzing Children's Art.* San Francisco, CA: National Press Books.

Kernberg, O. (1967). Borderline personality organization. *Journal of the American Psychoanalytic Association, 15,* 641–685.

Kessler, J. W. (1966). *Psychopathology of Childhood.* Englewood Cliffs, New Jersey: Prentice Hall Inc.

Koch, C. (1952). *The Tree Test.* New York: Grune & Stratton.

Koch, M. (1980). Sexual abuse in children. *Adolescence, 15*(59), 643–648.

Kohut, H. (1966). Forms and transformations of narcissism. In P. H. Ornstein (Ed.), *The Search for the Self: Vol. 2* (pp. 427–460). New York: International Universities Press.

Kohut, H. (1972). Thoughts on narcissism and narcissistic rage. *Psychoanalytic Study of the Child, 27,* 360–400. New Haven: Yale University Press.

Kotkov, B., & Goodman, M. (1953). The Draw-a-Person tests of obese women. *Journal of Clinical Psychology, 9*(45), 362–364.

Koppitz, E. (1968). *Psychological Evaluation of Children's Human Figure Drawings.* New York: Grune & Stratton.

Krystal, H. (1968). *Massive Psychic Trauma.* New York: International Universities Press, Inc.

Krystal, H. (1978). Trauma and affects. *Psychoanalytic Study of the Child, 33,* 81–116. New Haven: Yale University Press.

Krystal, H. (1988). *Intergration and Self-Healing.* New Jersey: The Analytic Press.

Krystal, H., & Niederland, W. (1971). Psychic traumatization. Boston: *International Psychiatry Clinics, 8* (1).

Landisberg, S. (1969). The use of the H-T-P in a mental hygiene clinic for children. In J. N. Buck & E. F. Hammer (Eds.), *Advances in the House-Tree-Person Technique: Variations and Applications.* Los Angeles: Western Psychological Services.

Levick, M. (1983). *They Could Not Talk and So They Drew.* Springfield, IL: Charles C Thomas.

Levine, A., & Sapolsky A. (1969). The use of the H-T-P as an aid in the screening of hospitalized patients. In J. N. Buck & E. F. Hammer (Eds.), *Advances in the House-Tree-Person technique: Variations and Applications.* Los Angeles, CA: Western Psychological Services.

Levy, S. (1950). Figure drawing as a projective test. In L. E. Abt & L. Bellack (Eds.), *Projective Psychology* (pp. 257–297). New York: Knopf.

Lieske, A. M. (1981). Incest: An overview. *Perspectives in Psychiatric Care, 29*(2), 59–63.

Lowenfeld, V., & Brittain W. (1975). *Creative and Mental Growth.* New York: Macmillan.

Lowenfeld, V., & Brittain, W. (1982). *Creative Mental Growth* (7th ed.). New York: Macmillan.

Lyons, J. (1955). The scar on the H-T-P tree. *Journal of Clinical Psychology, 11,* 267–270.

MacFarlane, K., Waterman, J., Conerly, S., Damon, L., Durfee, M., & Long, S. (1986). *Sexual Abuse of Young Children*. New York: The Guilford Press.

Machover, K. (1949). *Personality Projection in the Drawings of the Human Figure*. Springfield, IL: Charles C Thomas.

Machover, K. (1980). *Personality Projection in the Drawing of the Human Figure*. Springfield, IL: Charles C Thomas.

Maisch, H. (1972). *Incest* (C. Bearne, Trans.). New York: Stein & Day.

Maltz, W., & Holman, B. (1987). *Incest and Sexuality*. Springfield, MA: Lexington Books.

Markham, S. (1954). An item analysis of children's drawings of a house. *Journal of Clinical Psychology, 10*, 185–187.

Marzolf, S. S., & Kirchner, J. H. (1972). House-Tree-Person drawings and personality traits. *Journal of Personality Assessment, 36*, 148–165.

Matarazzo, J. (1980). *Wechsler's Measurement and Appraisal of Adult Intelligence*. New York: Oxford University Press.

McCarthy, S. (1924). *Children's Drawings*. Baltimore: Williams & Wilkins.

Meiselman, K. (1978). *Incest: A Psychological Study of Causes and Effects with Treatment Recommendations*. San Francisco: Jossey-Bass.

Minuchin, S. (1974). *Families and Family Therapy*. Cambridge, MA: Harvard University Press.

Minuchin, S. (1981). *Family Therapy Techniques*. Cambridge, MA: Harvard University Press.

Mitchell, S. (1988). *Relational Concepts in Psychoanalysis: An Integration*. Cambridge, MA: Harvard University Press.

Mrazek, P., & Kempe, H. C. (1981). *Sexually Abused Children and Their Families*. Oxford, England: Pergamon Press.

Murphy, W. F. (1958). Character trauma and sensory perception. *International Journal of Psychoanalysis, 40*, 94–104.

Mursell, G. R. (1969). The use of the H-T-P with the mentally deficient. In J. N. Buck & E. F. Hammer (Eds.), *Advances in the House-Tree-Person Technique: Variations and Applications*. Los Angeles, CA: Western Psychological Services.

Ochberg, F. (1988). *Post-Traumatic Therapy and Victims of Violence*. New York: Brunner/Mazel.

Ogdon, D. (1977). *Psychodiagnostics and Personality Assessment: A Handbook, Second Edition*. Los Angeles, CA: Western Psychological Services.

Peller, L. (1954, June). *Libidinal phases, ego development and play*. Paper presented at the meeting of the New York Psychoanalytic Society, New York.

Peters, J. J. (1978). Children who are victims of sexual assault and the psychology of offenders. *American Journal of Psychotherapy, 30*, 398–421.

Piaget, J. (1962). *Play, Dreams, and Imitation in Childhood*. New York: Norton.

Piaget, J. (1979). *Intelligence and Affectivity: Their Relationship During Child Development*. Palo Alto, CA: Annual Reviews, Inc.

Pine, F. (1982). The experience of self. *Psychoanalytic Study of the Child, 37*, 143–160. New Haven: Yale University Press.

Plaut, E. (1979). Play and adaptation. *Psychoanalytic Study of the Child, 34*, 217–231. New Haven: Yale University Press.

Redl, F., & Wineman, D. (1957). *The Aggressive Child*. New York: The Free Press.

Reich, A. (1973). Pathological forms of self-esteem regulation. In *Annie Reich* (pp. 288–311). New York: International Universities Press.

Reich, A. (1979). Pathologic forms of self-esteem regulation. *Psychoanalytic Study of the Child, 1985*, 215–232. New Haven: Yale University Press.

Ross, C., Norton, G. R., & Wozney, K. (1989). Multiple personality disorder: An analysis of 236 cases. *Canadian Journal of Psychiatry, 34*(5), 413–418.

Rouma, G. (1913). *The Child's Graphic Language*. Paris: Mich. et Thron.

Rubin, J. (1976). *Child Art Therapy*. New York: Jason Aronson.

Rubin, J. (1984). *Child Art Therapy*. New York: Van Nostrand Reinhold Co.

Sarnoff, C. (1976). *Latency*. New York: Jason Aronson.

Schildkrout, M., Shenker, I. R., & Sonnenblick, M. (1972). *Human Figure Drawings in Adolescents*. New York: Brunner/Mazel.

Seligman, M. E. (1975). *Helplessness*. San Francisco: W. H. Freeman & Company.

Sgroi, S. (1982). *Handbook of Clinical Intervention in Child Sexual Abuse*. Springfield, MA: Lexington Books.

Sgroi, S. (1988). *Vulnerable Populations*. Springfield, MA: Lexington Books.

Shapiro S. (1987). Self-mutilation and self-blame in incest victims. *American Journal of Psychotherapy, 16*(1), 46–54.

Shengold, L. (1979). Child abuse and deprivation: Soul murder. *Journal of the American Psychoanalytic Association, 27,* 533–559.

Shengold, L. (1980). Some reflections on a case of mother/adolescent son incest. *International Journal of Psychoanalysis, 61,* 461–476.

Shneidman, E. S. (1958). Some relationships between thematic and drawing materials. In E. F. Hammer (Ed.), *The Clinical Application of Projective Drawings* (pp. 620–627). Springfield, IL: Charles C Thomas.

Sidun, N., & Rosenthal, R. (1987). Graphic indicators of sexual abuse in Draw-A-Person tests of psychiatrically hospitalized adolescents. *The Arts in Psychotherapy, 14,* 25–33.

Stafford, C. D. (1972). *What Freud Really Said*. New York: Schocken Books.

Summit, R. (1983). The child sexual abuse accommodation syndrome. *Child Abuse and Neglect, 7,* 177–193.

Summit, R., & Kryso, J. (1978). Sexual abuse of children: A clinical spectrum. *American Journal of Orthopsychiatry 48*(2), 237–250.

Symonds, M. (1966). The depressions in childhood and adolescence. *The American Journal of Psychoanalysis, 28*(2), 189–195.

Terr, L. C. (1984). Time and trauma. *Psychoanalytic Study of the Child, 39,* 633–665. New Haven: Yale University Press.

Terr, L. (1989). Treating Psychic Trauma in Children: A preliminary discussion. *Journal of Traumatic Stress, 2*(1), 3–20.

Tolpin, M. (1971). On the beginnings of a cohesive self. An application of the concept of transmuting internalizations to the study of the transitional object and signal anxiety. *Psychoanalytic Study of the Child, 26,* 316–351. New Haven: Yale University Press.

Ulman, R. B., & Brothers, D. (1988). *The Shattered Self*. New Jersey: The Analytic Press.

Urban, W. H. (1963). *The Draw-A-Person Catalogue for Interpretive Analysis*. Los Angeles, CA: Western Psychological Services.

U.S. Department of Health and Human Services, National Center on Child Abuse and Neglect (1979/1981). *Child Sexual Abuse: Incest Assault and Sexual Exploitation*. (DHHS Publication No. [OHDS] 81-30166), issued 1979, revised 1981.

van der Kolk, B. (1987). *Psychological Trauma*. Washington, DC: American Psychiatric Press.

Waelder, R. (1933). The psychoanalytic theory of play. *Psychoanalytic Quarterly, 11.*

Waigandt, A., Wallace, D., Philps, L., & Miller, D. (1990). The impact of sexual assault on physical health status. *Journal of Traumatic Stress, 3*(1), 93–102.

White, M., & Weiner, M. (1986). *The Theory and Practice of Self Psychology*. New York: Brunner/Mazel.

Williams, G., & Wood, M. (1977). *Developmental Art Therapy*. Baltimore: University Park Press.

Williams, M. (1987). Reconstruction of an early seduction and its aftereffects. *Journal of the American Psychoanalytic Association, 35,* 145–163.

Wohl, A., & Kaufman, B. (1985). *Silent Screams and Hidden Cries: An Interpretation of Artwork by Children from Violent Homes*. New York: Brunner/Mazel.

Yates, A. (1982). Children eroticized by incest. *American Journal of Psychiatry, 139*(4), 482–485.

INDEX